UKRAIN
UNITED STATES.

Unexpected Ways Two Nations Affected Each Other

Andy Lazko

U-Krane
Copyright © Andy Lazko
Published: March 2018
Paperback ISBN: 9781980477150
eBook ASIN: B07B8474M1

Table of Contents

..

Introduction

While studying, working and travelling in the United States, I often encountered people who, after inquiring about where I was from and hearing the answer "Ukraine", immediately asked the next question - "Isn't it the same as Russia?"

Surprisingly, the only place where people knew that Ukraine is not Russia for sure, was the New York Stock Exchange, which the author had a lucky opportunity to visit. That knowledge may be explained by the influential Ukrainian Diaspora in that city I guess. The same holds true for Chicago also, not just because of the same Diaspora there, but also because the "hottest neighborhood" in the US, according to Redfin, in 2016 was named the Chicago's Ukrainian Village.

No. Two absolutely different nations! Even more different than England and Scotland or Ireland. And the strife for the independence of Ukraine from Russia is probably more lasting and severe than the fight for independence of Scotland from England, as portrayed in the famous Mel Gibson's movie "Braveheart".

Actually, this confusion between Ukraine and Russia is what Russia has wanted to achieve for centuries - it needed and still needs Ukraine's history, Ukraine's traditions, culture and even language. Among other things, it is in the habit of appropriating achievements created by Ukrainians.

The United States is a great country because of its entrepreneurial spirit of people of different nationalities - Italians (I think of Lee Iacocca here), Germans, French, Jews. The country did not suppress the individuals' national identities and even encouraged them to be American-Italians, American-Jewish, American-Germans, etc.

The reader of this book may find it interesting to learn in what sometimes unexpected ways Ukrainians (wrongfully called Russians by the way) have affected the United States and how the United States in its turn has affected the destiny of the Great Cossack Nation Ukraine is.

PROLOGUE

Vikings, Cossacks on the Dnieper, Kiev Queen of France

"In 1492, the year Christopher Columbus landed on the Caribbean island he named San Salvador and King Ferdinand and Queen Isabella signed a decree expelling the Jews from Spain, the Cossacks made their first appearance in the international arena. According to a complaint sent that year to Grand Duke Alexander of Lithuania by the Crimean khan, subjects of the duke from the cities of Kiev and Cherkasy had captured and pillaged a Tatar ship in what seems to have been the lower reaches of the Dnieper. The duke never questioned that these might be his people or that they might have engaged in steppe-style highway robbery. He ordered his borderland (the term he used was "Ukrainian") officials to investigate the Cossacks who might have been involved in the raid. He also ordered that the perpetrators be executed and that their belongings, which apparently had to include the stolen merchandise, be given to a representative of the khan.

If Alexander's orders were carried out, they had no lasting effect. In the following year, the Crimean khan accused Cossacks from Cherkasy of attacking a Muscovite ambassador. In 1499, Cossacks were spotted at the Dnieper estuary ravaging the environs of the Tatar fortress at Ochakiv...

To stop Cossack expeditions going down the Dnieper to the Black Sea, the khan considered blocking the Dnieper near Ochakiv with chains",

1

starts one of the chapters of his book "Gates of Europe: History of Ukraine" Harvard Professor Serhii Plokhy.

Why did Crimean khan complain about Ukrainian Cossacks to Lithuanian king? Who were the Muscovites and why their ambassador traveled to Crimea? What value could that ambassador have had on him so that the Cossacks decided to capture it?

To get the answers and the bigger picture, we need to make a quick tour back some 600 years before the event and discover how the most powerful and large Kingdom of Medieval Europe was founded and what the Vikings have to do with it.

In the summer of year 860 A.D. Vikings flotilla came down the Dnieper (Dnipro) river (the river that flows from north to the south dividing current Ukraine in half), crossed the Black Sea and attacked the city of Constantinople. Thus the shortest route from the Baltic Sea to the Black one was made. A bit later it will be extended and be called "the Trade Route from the Varangians to the Greeks".

They were the Rus' Vikings, a conglomerate of Swedish, Norwegian and Finnish Norsemen with the word "rus" meaning in Scandinavian "men who row".

The leader of that first recorded military campaign on Byzantium was Kiev Prince Askold. There were 360 boats in the flotilla with 8 000 warriors on them. To prevent the seizure of the city, the ruler of Constantinople offered peace, granted Askold the title equal to that of an Emperor or a King and to sanctify all that, Askold and part of his warriors were baptized into Christianity.

In 866 Patriarch Photios wrote that Rus had accepted Christianity and was performing Christian rituals. It means that Kiev had a Christian church in the ninth century and was a metropolis of the Ecumenical Pariarchate already in that time.

2

In the year 882, with the Dnieper River becoming such a lucrative trade artery, two Viking clans start competing for the best possible hub on the route - the city of Kiev.

Kiev was founded in 482, so it had been a large city already by the time Vikings came to it 400 hundred years later.

Situated on the hills, well positioned for defenses and almost half the road from Scandinavia to Constantinople, it presented strategic advantage to the ones who controlled it.

That very year on behalf of the house Rurik a Viking chieftain HELGI (Oleh as a Slavic version of the name in the chronicles) captured Kiev and killed Askold who was even some relative to Helgi by some sources. It may be hard to believe, but the Askold's grave situated on the hill overseeing the Dnieper river downtown current capital of Ukraine is still there attracting thousands of visitors each year.

In the year 945, Ingvar (Ihor), Helgi's successor was killed by a local East Slavic tribe while collecting the tribute. It was one of the several Slavic tribes that would constitute the future state.

The prince of the tribe proposed to Ingvar's widow whose name was HELGA (Olha).

Helga tricked the prince to Kiev and had him killed on the boat. The other group of matchmakers was scalded to death in the Scandinavian steam bath.

She was the first ruler of the land to accept Christianity, so the Orthodox Church considers her equal to a saint.

972. SVEINALD (Sviatoslav) was only 3 when his mother Helga became a widow. To the ancestors and up to our days he will be known as "the BRAVE" because he spent almost all his life in different battles across Southern Europe while his mother reigned in Kiev. Sveinald was killed returning home to Kiev from Byzantium on the Dnieper

river rapids close to the place where the current city of Zaporizhia is situated.

Sveinald's figure is important to historians and to our narrative, since he is the first of the dynasty there is a physical description of. It was made by the Byzantine chronicler Leo the Deacon who met Sveinald in person during the Kiev King's trip to Constantinople.

According to the Deacon's description, the Kiev King was broad-shouldered, of medium height with blue eyes and short wide nose. He had a bushy long mustache but his beard was cleanly shaven. His head was also shaven with one lock of blond hair untouched which was a sign of noble origin.

Another thing that drew the chronicler's attention was that Sveinald rowed equally with his men and the only things that made him stand out from his subjects were white clean clothes and a gold earring in one of his ears. There is a powerful monument to Sveinald at the place of his death near Zaporizhia conveying all these features.

Very important for the European history is the year 980 when VLADIMIR "the GREAT", who was born out of wedlock of Sveinald and one of his courtesans, becomes Kiev king.

Since he was a bastard son, initially he had been sent to the farthest province of Kiev Rus - city of Novgorod (situated in current Russia), while Sveinald's two other sons stayed in Kiev.

With the death of their father Sveinald, one of the brothers who stayed in Kiev killed another and Vladimir had to flee to Scandinavia to save his life. He had to stay in his ancestral fortress for 5 years while collecting forces. Later, with his Viking uncle's military support he returned to Kiev Rus and took the Kiev throne from his brother.

With all the military support Vladimir now had, he presented a serious power on the European map.

"With insurrections troubling Byzantium, the emperor Basil II (976–1025) sought military aid from Vladimir, who agreed, in exchange for Basil's sister Anne in marriage. A pact was reached about 987 when Vladimir also consented to the condition that he become a Christian. Having undergone baptism, assuming the Christian patronal name Basil, he stormed the Byzantine area of Chersonesus (Korsun, now part of Sevastopol, Crimea) to eliminate Constantinople's final reluctance. Vladimir then ordered the Christian conversion of Kiev and Novgorod, "describes the events Encyclopedia Britannica.

Kiev Rus Christianization took place in 988 in Kiev and there is a monument to Vladimir on one of the Kiev hills across the place on the Dnieper River where that mass Christianization most likely took place.

Later historians would compare Vladimir's baptism to Emperor Constantine's establishing Christianity as the official religion of the Roman Empire.

During that period of time, Kiev became the place where many Europe's historic figures spent time.

For example, legendary Norwegian king Olav Tryggvason spent many years in Kiev during his exile.

The future King of Norway Magnus the Good also spent some years in Kiev for military training education.

1019. YAROSLAV "The WISE" starts his rule.

With his father Vladimir marrying into the Byzantium imperial family, two countries became the allies and Kiev started the process of emulating all the best there was in Byzantium.

King Yaroslav was good at learning (the contemporaries wrote that he was reading "day and night") and building. Many wonderful cathedrals he built in Kiev and stand to our days have resemblance with the ones in Constantinople by the way.

Kiev and the whole country of Rus were flourishing and King Yaroslav used the opportunity to strengthen the influence on other European states. He did so via marriage.

Yaroslav himself married a daughter of Swedish King Olaf Ericsson.

In the royal Viking city of Sigtuna which was the childhood home of the Swedish princess Ingegerd Olofsdotter, the future wife of Yaroslav the Wise, recently a lot of Kiev Rus necklaces and ceramics have been uncovered.

Yaroslav's first daughter Yelizaveta (Scandinavian name - Ellisiv) married the King of Norway Harald Hardraada. And what a story of marriage it was!

After Yaroslav the Wise refused Harald to marry away Elizabeth, Harald left for Constantinople and returned to Kiev with glory and treasures. The marriage took place in 1045, and next year the newlywed went to Norway.

One more year later, in 1047 King Harald Hardrade became the King of Norway and the same year founded a new capital of Norway - Oslo, turning the city into the new royal residence. Harald will die in 1066 at the Battle of Britain with his Kiev wife waiting for his return at the Orkney Islands.

Yaroslav's another daughter, Anna will become the famous Queen of France.

Unlike her husband, the King Henry I of France, Anne could read and write, and, what is interesting to learn, in her letters to her father she described Paris as a gloomy place which could not be even closely compared to Kiev.

These are some unique events in the history of France connected with Anna's name:

- Queen Ann of Kiev (Anne de Kiev) was the first to use name Philip ("lover of horses") in the history of French Kings names.

- When her husband King Henry I died, Queen Ann became the first reagent to solely rule France until Philip reached maturity.

- Anna's signature in Cyrillic on a French royal charter is the only known example of a Capetian dynasty queen's signature on parchment and the only known (pre-13th century) signature of a member of the Rurikid dynasty.

- The unique Reims Gospel all the French Kings swore allegiance on was brought to Paris from Kiev and first several pages in Cyrillic are believed to be handwritten by Anne herself and thus present the oldest extant example of Old Ukrainian handwriting.

A medieval fresco depicting Anne of Kiev, her mother, and two sisters is preserved in Kiev's Saint Sophia Cathedral.

Two 20th-century full-figure sculptures of Anne are found in Senlis near Paris in the church of Saint Vincent's Monastery, which she had founded.

(Current Russia tried numerous times to call Anne of Kiev "theirs" with the last public attempt made by Putin during his meeting with the newly elected President of France Macron. Luckily, President Macron knew history well and gave his reply to Putin's claim during his meeting with the President of Ukraine telling that he views Anne of Kiev as a symbol of relations between France and Ukraine.

We will address this subject in the following chapters, but as of now there are only two numbers to look at - 1075 is the year Queen Ann died, 1272* - is the year when the Mongolian Khan Mengu-Timur turns a small wooden Meryan village on the swamps called Moskva into an administrative center of the Golden Horde. There is the Swampy (Bolotnaya) Squire right in the center of Moscow on the other side of Kremlin from the Red one. Haze and terrible smell of sulfur dioxide that covers the current Moscow from time to time, means that the swamp is still there. Ukrainians make a caustic joke on that account telling that sulfur is a sure telltale sign of the presence of some evil creature from the horror books and movies.)

In 1043 King Yaroslav was already so powerful, that he sent his flotilla from Kiev to demand money from Byzantium.

Constantinople refused, tried to withstand, but gets its flotilla defeated. The seizure of the city is prevented only by the huge storm.

This last episode clearly shows what might military and politically Kiev had by the middle of the 11th century.

If there is theoretically any city which had the right to claim to be called '"The Third Rome", - it is Kiev of that time. (Actually, according to UNESCO, the Kiev Saint Sophia Cathedral mentioned above, was "designed to rival Hagia Sophia in Constantinople.., and symbolized 'New Constantinople', capital of Christian principality of Kiev.")

Kiev of those days was several times larger than Paris or London. Much more magnificent also. And King Yaroslav the Wise was the most influential ruler in Europe.

"By territory, what is the biggest kingdom in Medieval Europe?

1. France

2. England

3. Germany (German Empire)

4. Byzantium (Roman Empire)

5. None of the above,"

- asks his readers Christian Raffensperger, Associate Professor of History at Wittenberg University. And answers himself:

"If you answered "5" you are correct! While England and France are the two most well studied medieval kingdoms among American and Anglophone medievalists, they are not the largest by territory. This is despite the specificity they get on maps in modern textbooks. It is also not the German Empire which did cover a swath of central medieval Europe. Nor is it the Byzantine (Roman) Empire which for most of the Middle Ages was shrinking, not growing, in territory – despite the best efforts of Basil II.

The correct answer to the question is: the kingdom of Rus'. "What?" you may say or perhaps "Where?" Both are valid questions because not only was Rus' the largest kingdom in medieval Europe it is also the most unknown."

So what happened to this powerful Kiev Rus state?

The most painful wound to it was inflicted by the Asian military superpower of those days - the Golden Horde in the year 1240 A.D.

Kiev chose to fight, lost, but probably saved other countries of Europe by weakening the military power of the Horde.

Kiev was weakened too, so the center moved to Lithuania and later on to Poland which formed the Polish-Lithuanian Commonwealth of which the remnants of the Kiev Rus became an integral part. It's worth mentioning that current Belarus was also part of the Commonwealth.

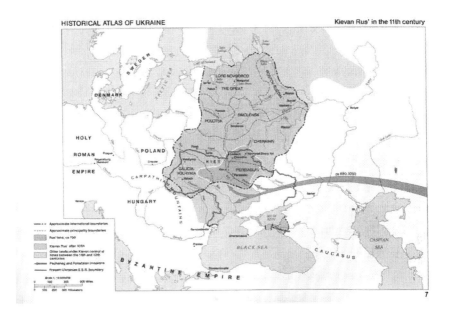

It is after that Horde invasion, the Dnieper and adjacent to it territories started to be perceived as a defending barrier from nomads. These lands became borderland, defending edge of the civilization. That is how term "Ukraine" came into existence.

Living in those lands was truly like living on the edge - one had to know how to defend himself or herself to survive - very similar to the American Wild West several centuries later.

Only in Ukraine, they were called the Cossacks, and in the States, they will be the Cowboys.

To the opposite of this situation, another story was to the north of Kiev.

Totally different realm to that of the Commonwealth.

The city of Moscow which was founded only some 100 years after the most glorious days of Kiev Rus, chose to serve the Golden Horde by collecting tribute from its realm for the Horde. It delivered the tribute first to the Golden Horde via the Volga River for 200 years and later to the Crimean khan for another 250 years.

The realm controlled by Moscow wore the official name of MUSCOVY, - Moscow itself used that name while signing a Treaty with the Polish-Lithuanian Commonwealth in 1449, while the Commonwealth signed as "Rus."

That was the Muscovite ambassador going to Crimea the Cossacks attacked in 1493 mentioned in the beginning of the Prologue.

It is very important to grasp the meaning of the fact of the Muscovy being an aggressive servant for Golden Horde and Crimean khan for so long, because it explains a lot of what is going on even in current Russia.

It affected the language, customs, and political structure.

It shows itself in the psychology of grasping, taking away what does not belong to you. It is in the servitude to the superior power or will. It is the same disrespect to the lives of the same kind. Inability and unwillingness to work and create something on one's own.

In short, Ukraine and Muscovy were two absolutely different realms for centuries:

Ukraine-Rus was part and defender of the European civilization;

Muscovy-Russia – part of the Asian one.

(*) The details of how and by whom Moscow was founded together with the other historic insights are given in the chapters at the very end of this book.

1. Ukrainian Hetman, Lord Byron, American Highest-Paid Actress of the Time

Hetman in not the same as hitman, although...

16th and 17th centuries were the power centuries for the Cossacks - despite constant wars and battles, their ranks grew immensely.

Their headquarters became an island amidst Dnieper rapids near the place, where 500 years before, the Kiev King Sveinald/Sviatoslav the Brave was killed.

The name of the island was Khortytsia, and the name of the fortress on that island - Sich (which some of the readers might connect to one of the best world producers of engines for the planes and helicopters - Motor Sich).

What is also interesting, the Cossacks that chose that place for their headquarters even looked the same and behaved in a similar way as Sveinald: they also shaved their beards but grew mustaches. They shaved their heads but left the forelocks of hair. The neighboring nations started calling them after that piece of hair - "Forelocks" – *Hohols* in Ukrainian.

Also, just like Sveinald/Sviatoslav, they acted like equal among equals and the leaders they chose for themselves were elected by means of an open vote. Example of direct democracy in those days.

The leaders chosen were usually highly experienced, wise and smart men, proven warriors in many battles. They were called Hetmans. Some Hetmans were highly educated, speaking several languages with some education from Kiev which was becoming an educational powerhouse of Eastern Europe in those days already.

If there was a contemporary example of such ingenious warriors, for American readers it would be the renown Richard Marcinko, a man with a surprisingly Ukrainian last name (-nko) and with ancestral roots in Slovakia, a little also Slavic country bordering on Ukraine. "Rogue warriors" would also be a perfect phrase to describe the Cossacks. One only wonders if some of Richard's ancestors had been the Sich Cossacks too.

The Cossacks also built longboats, they called "Chaika" (seagull) which in many ways resembled those of the Vikings and followed the same routs the Vikings used already 600 years earlier.

They pillaged the suburbs of the former Constantinople which became Istanbul by that time. They stormed the Ottoman fortresses like Varna and Trabzon.

They burnt almost all the Ottoman fleet near Crimea.

They attacked the largest slave market of Kaffa, situated in current day Feodosia in Crimea and freed all the slaves.

"The French ambassador in Istanbul, Count Philippe de Harlay of Сйsy, wrote to King Louis XIII in July 1620, "Every time the Cossacks are near here on the Black Sea, they seize incredible booty despite their weak forces and have such a reputation that strokes of the cudgel are required to force the Turkish soldiers to do battle against them on several galleys that the grand seigneur [the sultan] sends there with great difficulty", - writes Serhii Plokhy in the same book mentioned in the Prologue.

Together with Polish forces, they saved Vienna from the Turks invasion.

One of the most famous pieces of art conveying the spirit of the Cossackdom is the painting by the famous Ukrainian painter Ilya Repin: "Reply of the Zaporozhian Cossacks to the Turkish Sultan."

Before writing that portrait Ilya Repin studied the life of the Cossacks and concluded: "All that Gogol wrote about them is true! A holy people! No one in the world held so deeply freedom, equality, and fraternity.

The same painter also portrayed the reality of the Muscovite realm on the Volga river in the painting "Barge Haulers on the Volga". One can easily compare the two worlds.

In 1618, a Ukrainian Cossack army of 20 000 took part with the Polish forces in the siege of Moscow. It ended with Moscow accepting the terms of the Polish and the Cossacks' terms with Ukraine receiving back the city of Chernihiv which would become one of the Cossacks' strongholds.

Unfortunately for the future of the Commonwealth, Polish nobility crossed the line in how they treated Ukrainian peasants and Ukrainian Cossacks.

As a result, in 1648 there was a huge uprising against Poland led by Hetman Bohdan Khmelnitsky, whose property had been stolen and son murdered by a Polish official before the events.

In 1654, Khmelnitsky had to sign the Alliance with Muscovy to wage the war on Poland.

The telling episode of how different Muscovy was from Ukraine is the fact that Khmelnitsky, who spoke several languages, did not understand the Muscovy dialect and had to have the Muscovite ambassadors' letters translated into Latin so he could read them.

Muscovy, of course, almost immediately broke the Agreement and 13 years later signed Truce of Andrusovo with Poland dividing Ukraine in half by the Dnieper river. Under that agreement, Muscovy received the Left Bank Ukraine (to the East from the Dnieper) which will eventually wear the name of "Little Russia".

Poland kept the Right Bank Ukraine.

Near the end of that century, Ukrainian Cossacks had a Hetman whose name will be known all over Europe and later on around the world. His name was Ivan Mazepa and he had an extremely bright personality. Well-educated in Kiev, Warsaw and Italy, he spoke freely several languages and had an outgoing charismatic nature.

He restored churches, built educational institutions and was known on European political scene to the extent that even French Voltaire admired him.

In the beginning, Mazepa was on good terms with Peter the First to the extent that some contemporaries considered this kind of relationship as a friendship.

But after Peter decided to restrict the Cossacks' rights thus further violating previous agreements, Ivan Mazepa chose to take the side of Swedish Army of King Karl XII against Peter's Army in the crucial battle under Ukrainian city of Poltava.

That dramatic battle became a black day for the Swedish Army and the Swedish dominance on the continent.

And Mazepa even had to flee Ukraine.

But the power of his personality and his and Ukraine's drama was so strong, that more than a century later British poet Lord Byron devoted one of his most famous poems to him.

It is called "Mazeppa" and it starts with the description of the Poltava battle:

'Twas after dread Poltuwa's day,

When fortune left the royal Swede--

Around a slaughtered army lay,

No more to combat and to bleed.

The power and glory of the war,

Faithless as their vain votaries, men,

Had passed to the triumphant Czar,

And Moscow's walls were safe again--

Until a day more dark and drear,

And a more memorable year,

17

Should give to slaughter and to shame

A mightier host and haughtier name;

A greater wreck, a deeper fall,

A shock to one--a thunderbolt to all.

-

Later in the poem, Lord Byron mentions an instance in Ivan Mazeppa's young life, namely his affair with a Polish Countess Theresa during his days as a page at the Court of King John II Casimir Vasa.

Countess Theresa was married to a much older Count. On learning of the affair, the Count tied Mazepa naked to a wild horse and set the horse loose.

'Bring forth the horse!' The horse was brought;

In truth, he was a noble Steed,

A Tartar of the Ukraine breed,

Who looked as though the Speed of thought

Were in his limbs – but he was wild,

Wild as the wild-deer, and untaught,

With spur and bridle undefiled;42

'Twas but a day he had been caught,

And snorting with erected mane

And struggling fiercely but in vain,

In the full foam of wrath and dread,

To me, the Desert-born was led. –

They bound me on, that menial throng,

Upon his back with many a thong,

Then loosed him with a sudden lash

Away! – Away! – and on we dash! –

Torrents less rapid and less rash.

-

The poem almost immediately became a theater performance and at once became an unbelievable success - after its first season in 1831, the play ran for several hundred performances at Astley's Royal Amphitheatre in London.

It was revived numerous times many years subsequently in both England and later in America.

But the most famous production was the one that starred the celebrated Adah Isaacs Menken, an American actress, who played the role of Mazeppa for American audiences in 1861 and for English audiences two years later to great acclaim.

In fact, Adah Isaacs Menken became the highest earning actress of her time mostly because of her performance in this melodrama, where she played young Ukrainian hetman with a climax that featured her apparently nude and riding a horse on stage.

Lord Byron was not the only one inspired by the life of Ivan Mazepa by the way - Piotr Chaikovsky composed opera "Mazeppa", Franz List - symphonic opera with the same name, Victor Hugo wrote a poem, Voltaire devoted a lot of attention to the personality of Ivan Mazepa in his "History of Charles XII of Sweden."

-

- "Mazeppa" by Louis Guisnet, 1874

<u>Pruth Campaign</u>

The story had continuation which should be at least briefly mentioned. After the Poltava defeat, the wounded Charles XII of Sweden and stayed in Moldova which was under the protection of the Ottomans. Mazepa died in the fall of the same year near the city of Bendery and Peter I kept on sending demands for the sultan to give Charles XII to him which the sultan ignored. A year later, Peter I set a specific date when he expected the sultan's reply, which Ahmed III took for ultimatum and declared war on Muscovy.

It was a good thing for the Crimean Khan who, as the author of a Pulitzer prize-winning book Peter the Great Robert Massie writes, "had been stripped of his right to tribute from Russia by the treaty of 1700."

One should probably pause here and imagine this well-hidden fact that Muscovy, future "Russia", paid tribute to the Crimean khans until 1700 including Peter I himself.

"The Tsar was reduced to paying an annual sum to the Khan, protection money which the Khan called a tribute and the Russians preferred to describe as a gift…"

Dositheus, the Orthodox Patriarch of Jerusalem sent Peter I a "singing jibe": "The Crimean Tatars are but a handful, and yet they boast that they receive tribute from you. The Tatars are Turkish subjects, so it follows that you are Turkish subjects."

"The most prominent was the violent Russophobe Khan of the Crimea, Devlet Gerey, who had been stripped of his right to tribute from Russia by the treaty of 1700."

It is a bit unusual in such a historic book to encounter phrases like "Russophobe Khan" because Muscovy had been paying tribute to the Crimean Khan for almost two centuries by that time already. The Crimean Khan was simply well aware of who he was dealing with, - his ancestor Devlet I Geray had to teach Ivan IV "The Terrible" a lesson by burning Moscow to the ground in 1571 for trying to cheat him.

But here in 1711 and after the Poltava Battle Peter I decided he was ready to attack the Ottoman empire first. His plans were very ambitious: "Against the Turks, Peter's plan, bold to recklessness, was to march to the lower Danube, cross the river just above the place where it flows into the Black Sea and proceed southwest through Bulgaria to a point where he could threaten the Sultan's second capital, Adrianople, and even the fabled city of Constantinople itself."

With his large army of veterans from Poltava, Peter I was so confident it would be an easy conquest, he even took his wife with him.

Yet, as soon as his army crossed Ukraine and entered Moldova, Ottomans demolished two-thirds of that army and forced the Tsar, Tsarina and the remains of their army of veterans into surrender near the Pruth River.

Robert Massie describes the reasons well in the following passage: "Could it have come to this? Yet, why not? Had not exactly the same thing happened to his enemy Charles (XII of Sweden)? And for identical reason: Too proud, too sure of his destiny, he had ventured too far onto enemy ground.

He was pinned down against a river and ringed by 300 cannon which could sweep his camp with shot and shell. Most important, his men were so exhausted by hunger and heat that some of them could no longer fight.

Actually, the situation was much worse than Charles': the Swedish army had not been surrounded by superior forces, and the King himself had found a way to escape... He, the Russian Tsar, the victor of Poltava, would be overwhelmed and perhaps pulled through the streets of Constantinople in a cage."

The conditions of the Grand Vizier turned out much milder than expected - Peter I was to demolish several Russian fortresses, return the city of Azov and Taganrog to the Turks, and dismantle the Black Sea fleet. Some historians insist that Peter I simply paid a sizable bribe to the Vizier of 500, 000 rubles from the State Treasury and not 150,000 of his wife's personal money as the book suggests.

Robert Massie writes that Tatar Khan wept in frustration when the Grand Vizier signed the peace treaty. Charles XII was also in disbelief. Both were confident that Mehmed Pasha made a strategic mistake by not taking Russian tsar to captivity.

Ukrainians surely agree with that, because humiliated Peter I on his way back to Moscow vented his anger by ordering the remains of his troops to plunder and burn several Ukrainian cities, such as Nemyriv and Bila Tserkva near Kiev.

2. Russian Vempire formation

Yes, with the "V."

Some six years before the Poltava battle, Peter the First started building the new capital for his country.

In 1703 Peter captured the Swedish city of Nyen at the mouth of the Neva River and almost immediately started building Saint Petersburg.

Many tourists who visit that city today and admire it, but simply do not know the truth about its construction -

The project of the city was made by the Swiss- Italian Domenico Trezzini. The chief architect was Frenchman Jean-Baptiste Alexandre Le Blond. That is why there is a French taste to its looks. But beneath all those buildings and canals there are piles of the human bones, because tens of thousands of conscripted peasants died building the city.

One wonders if there is any other city in the world history built on such terrible sacrifices.

Why did he call it Saint Petersburg? "Saint" is not a Russian word, "burg" is not a Russian ending.

Why move the capital right on the border anyway?

Seems like Peter's aspirations were solely towards Europe. He wanted to become equal among European kings and queens.

But how to become equal among European kings and queens with the Asian Muscovy's background?

So with changing the capital, he decided to rebrand (!) the whole country.

It took him almost twelve years after the Poltava battle to finish all the necessary preparations.

And in 1721 he did the following:

1. He proclaimed himself an Emperor.
2. He took the Dutch flag, changed the stripes order on it and called it the new Flag of his newly born Empire. It is the current Russian "tricolor".
3. Ordered to use name "Russia" instead of Muscovy in all documentation.

Of course to do the latter was the hardest since Moscow did not even exist in the times of the most glorious days of Kiev Rus.

A major effect of these actions was that history books were removed all over Ukraine and the whole history was brutally rewritten and a lot of events in Muscovy's history were simply made up.

Many Russians try to use Novgorod as the reason to claim a legacy of the whole Kiev Rus, because "Oleg-Helgi came to Kiev from Novgorod" and both Vladimir the Great and Yaroslav the Wise ruled in Novgorod before becoming kings in Kiev.

First, the whole Rurik dynasty was Scandinavian. The very fact that Vladimir had to flee from Novgorod and hide in Sweden from his brother clearly demonstrates the fact.

Second, Novgorod was one of many Princedoms and was in submission to Kiev to which it even paid tribute until the times of Yaroslav the Wise.

Third and the last, let us see how Moscow established a memorable bond with that city of Novgorod to claim legacy afterwards. *Encyclopedia Britannica* gives the following account of the events telling that

"Ivan the Terrible... was extremely unsuccessful in wars against Sweden and Poland... but he instituted the reign of terror against hereditary nobility. In 1570, for example, Ivan personally led his oprichniki troops against Novgorod, destroying that city and executing several thousand of its inhabitants. Many boyars and other members of the gentry perished during this period, some being publicly executed with calculated and symbolic cruelty."

And current Russians erect monuments to that sadistic ruler, not to Novgorod, which tells a lot of the spiritual legacy in itself.

One other fact needs to be mentioned though, that when one year later (1571) Crimean khan Devlet I Girey approached Moscow with his troops to demand the overdue tribute, Ivan the Terrible was nowhere to be found because he had fled Moscow in fear of his life.

So, Ivan the Terrible turned into Ivan the Terrified, and it is very symbolic of the behavior of the current "ivans", who are brutal and merciless to other people in their power, but turn into scared ones in the presence of the stronger and more determined force. The current relationships between Russia and one small Caucasian republic on which it has waged war twice in the past 30 years is a good example.

Disappointed and angered, the Crimean khan burnt Moscow to the ground.

The Westward expansion of the new Empire was more or less completed in the 60 years following Peter's death - during the reign of Tsaritsa Catherine II who annexed almost all the Duchy of Lithuania which would become today's Belarus with the city of Minsk in 1774.

And who was Tsaritsa Catherine by the way? Was she, at least, a product of Muscovy? The one who grew up in "Russia" and thus simply extended the wish of the "Russian nation" to move Westward?

Her original name was Sophie Friederike Auguste, Prinzessin von Anhalt-Zerbst, born April 21, 1729, Stettin, Prussia.

In 1815 Russia annexed Warsaw.

Historians now say that during that short period of time, as a result of annexation, Russia acquired the largest part of world Jewry and that there were more nobles of Polish culture in that Russian empire than there were nobles of the Russian culture.

There turned out to be more subjects of the tsar who could read and write the Polish language than Russian! Basically, this is how Muscovy dialect mutated into the contemporary Russian language - it was influenced by Polish and Ukrainian languages.

To remove any doubts that the so-called "Russian language" is a dialect of Ukrainian and not vice versa, it's sufficient to turn to the most authoritative lexicologists in this matter - Vladimir Dal, a Danish-German born in the territory of current Ukraine, in the city of Luhansk to be precise, currently occupied by Russia. His importance in the world was celebrated by a Google Doodle just recently on his birthday anniversary.

He wrote stories under the pen name of "Luhansk Cossack", but his major achievement was "Explanatory Dictionary of the Living Great Rusian Language" - with a single "S" on which Dal insisted. The Russians call it "unique spelling deviation from the standard grammar", but in fact, Dal was describing the language of Rusian people, people of Kiev Rus-Ukraine. The language in Muscovy-Russia he called a "dialect" of Rusian (Ukrainian, Ruthenian) language.

In fact, the whole trick of Peter I renaming his country into Russia was to confuse the two.

If it was to be described in modern business terms, it would be like, for example, the company "Adidas" suddenly having a rival firm selling similar-looking products under the brand-name "Abibas." People buy, but later see that a difference in two letters made them mistake one for another. It is exactly the same what Russia did.

It is done so not just to deceive the other nations, but also to get grounds to claim that history, language, and traditions of the current Ukraine are "theirs". The real reason behind Russia's aggression against Ukraine in the past 300 years including the current one is that country-"Abibas" is in a constant process of hostile takeover of the country-"Adidas", to continue the analogy. I

t does everything for the original one to disappear so that they could say they were the original one from the very beginning.

Returning back for a moment to Anne of Kiev, Queen of France.

Was she Rusenian (with a single "S"? Yes. She came to Paris from Rus being born in the capital of that most powerful state, the city of Kiev.

Was she Russian? Absolutely not! There was no country with such a name at the time.

Another proof that current Russia is in the process of hostile takeover of Kiev Rus history and an example of perverted logic is the reason Vladimir Putin named for annexation of Crimea from Ukraine. According to his words in his 2014 state of the nation address, Moscow annexed Crimea from Kiev, because Kiev King Vladimir was baptized there!

""It was in Crimea, in the ancient city of Chersonesus or Korsun, that Grand Prince Vladimir was baptised before bringing Christianity to Rus…this allows us to say that Crimea and Sevastopol have invaluable civilisational and even sacred importance for Russia," declared Putin.

Now slowly once again. Kiev King Vladimir was a grandfather to the future Queen of France Anne of Kiev. His baptism in Crimea took place in 988 which is 130 years before a small settlement on the bogs named Moscow was first mentioned. Some 1,000 years later Moscow annexes a territory from Kiev under pretense the event of baptism is more important to it than to Kiev or what? Light version of Crusade? More like marauding when Ukraine was weak, - said a famous Russian publicist Aleksandr Nevzorov.

Who brought civilization to whom - Kiev to Moscow or vice versa by the way?

Who educated whom? Who even at the beginning of the 18th century was a cultural center and who was on the periphery?

Quick case study.

Mohyla's Kiev Academy even after incorporation of Kiev by Muscovy, remained the largest educational institution in the tsar's domains.

This Academy's history is a good example of the "hostile merger" mentioned above.

This very Academy was opened in 1615. Another Ukrainian Academy - Ostroh was opened in 1576.

Moscow Academy of Science - 1724, Moscow University - 1755.

Some 150 years difference in education - an abyss even by those measures.

But in 1815 Moscow ordered to close Mohyla's Kiev Academy.

Why would any reasonable country want to close the largest and the oldest Academy in its realm? Actually, Russia closed almost all schools in Ukraine including Jesuit ones.

Russia knew where the true cultural and educational center was - in Kiev. How could it bear with the fact of educational inferiority? Without closing the Academy, how could Moscow be considered an educational center?

Without such a move, how would it be possible to forge the story about "Russia being elder and smarter brother to Ukraine"?

But let's look at the true products of Mohyla's Academy even in second and third generations:

One Petro Chaika was a graduate of the Mohyla's Academy. He came from a famous Ukrainian Cossacks clan and participated in the Poltava battle where he was wounded but survived. The Russian government sent him as a medic to the Vyatka region in the Urals. His grandson turned out gifted in music and would gradually become the world famous Piotr Chaikovsky. It is not clear where and when exactly Piotr decided to add "-ovsky" ending to his last name, but the truth remains.

After his 24th birthday, Piotr lived in Ukraine for several months almost every year. During this time he wrote more than 30 masterpieces using Ukrainian folklore and Taras Shevchenko's lyrics. In the times of persecution for the Ukrainian language (yes, Russia prohibited Ukrainian language multiple times and the reader can now guess why), he still used many Ukrainian folk songs in his works.

While in Kiev, he wrote operas such as "Koval" (Ukrainian for "smith"), "Vakula", "Mazepa" and "Cherry Garden by the House" together with "In the Garden by the River".

Fyodor Dostoyevsky - yes, the Russian icon is of Ukrainian origin. The Dostoyevsky family came from the Dostoyevo village which is near the Ukrainian-Belorussian border. One of the Dostoyevskys was a priest at Kiev-Pechersk (Cave) Monastery and even ran to become Metropolitan Bishop in 1647. The writer's grandfather, Andriy Dostoyevsky, was also a cleric and wanted his son Mikhail to become a cleric also. Mikhail chose to escape such destiny and ran off to St. Petersburgh where he became a famous surgeon, although in his youth he wrote poetry. It is important to know since here is what Fyodor Dostoyevsky's daughter wrote: "Poetic prowess was already in the

Ukrainian family of my father, and was not just given through my Moscow mother, as literature associates of Dostoyevsky suppose".

For those readers who want to compare how two nations differed, how different were the ways of life in Ukrainian village for example and in Russian, there is arguably no better writer than Nikolai Gogol, a Ukrainian (whom Russians appropriated of course already). His "Evenings on a Farm near Dikanka" is about Ukraine, and "Dead Souls" is about Russia.

He is the one who wrote the famous "Taras Bulba" about Ukrainian Cossacks and their struggle, which was filmed in Hollywood in 1962 starring Yul Brynner and Tony Curtis.

Maybe Ukrainian writers exaggerated something about Russian reality?

Russian poet Lermontov wrote:

Farewell, farewell, unwashed Russia,

The land of slaves, the land of lords,

And you, blue uniforms of gendarmes,

And you, obedient to them folks.

(Just a quick reminder that serfdom, basically slavery, was abolished in Russia in 1861 only to return in the form of the collective farms 60 years later).

Here is part of Sergei Yesenin's verse written in 1922 already.

Yesenin is considered as the one who knew "Russian soul" well, but married an American dancer Isadora Duncan nevertheless.

Gone for keeps, whereabouts are you stationed?

Are our rays shining brightly your way?
The sick bard medicates with potation
Great pox, picked up in far Kyrgyz plains.

These can neither be quelled nor placated.
Their rashness comes out of this blight.
You, Russeya of mine, Rus… seya…,
Is a land of the Asian side!

So, why such a title for this chapter?

Because by territory yes, Russia did qualify to be called Empire.

But by content...

When you compare it with other empires such as the British Empire, the French Empire, the Byzantine Empire, or the Roman Empire, one can see that there is something wrong or missing.

All the listed empires were of higher civilization, which eventually affected in a good way their colonies (education, medicine, roads, culture, etc.), and only Russia absorbed and occupied the smarter nations with higher civilization.

Contemporary Russian historian Yevgeniy Ponasenkov also singles out Russia telling that it is the only Empire with the extensive way of development.

Was it to any avail to it anyway? Apparently, new blood and brains did not change much in that realm, and only swole its arrogance.

Should Russia be compared to a person, it would be a bully, who comes to his neighbor's property, takes the result of other people's work and calls it his, "Russian."

Should Russia be compared to a popular fictional character, it would be a vampire.

But as a formation which basically takes the best wherever it comes, ruins everything and leaves desolated it looks like... the Golden Horde. Vampire of Civilization.

Note of Interest. There is a former ancient German city Konigsberg which currently belongs to Russia and wears a name after some communist - Kaliningrad. Although, the Potsdam Agreement placed it under Soviet administration and did not mention an explicit right of annexation, 100,000 remaining Germans were forcibly moved to Germany, and the city was repopulated with 400,000 Russians and other Soviet civilians.

And it is near that city there is the house in which Immanuel Kant, German philosopher, lived. It could be a great tourists' attraction, but here is the state in which the house has been just recently: It is a proper illustration of what happens to anything where current Russia comes.

3. John Paul Jones, Black Sea Cossacks, Crimea, Battle for Liman

John Paul Jones, a Revolutionary War hero known as the father of the U.S. Navy, left a mark in Ukraine's history. In the book *Life and Correspondence of John Paul Jones, Including his Narrative of the Campaign of the Liman* published in 1830 in New York and currently in the Library of Congress, the Admiral describes how and why he was invited to Russia and what happened there. Actually, the major events would be taking place on the territory of current Ukraine.

"War had been impending between Russia and the Porte, since the disturbances in the Crimea, in 1777, occasioned by the election of a Khan, in which the former interfered to support one of the candidates, with the ultimate view of dispossessing him entirely. The empress, encouraged by her eccentric and overbearing favorite and general, Potemkin, in the ambitious desire of being crowned at Constantinople, never lost sight of this intention." This first quote shows that Russian Empress Catherine had an ambitious desire to be crowned in Constantinople, and that "the invasion of the Crimea was determined upon, as a necessary preliminary to operations against Turkey." And it means that the Crimean invasion in itself was an intermediate goal. The ultimate plan had a totally different purpose – Constantinople.

"At the same time Potemkin and Suvorrof (Suvorov) subdued and received the homage of the tribes of the Kuban, and the extensive wilds more remote. A manifesto was published to justify these unprovoked acts and the annexation of those districts to the empire…By a new treaty the sovereignty of Russia over the Crimea, and a great part of Kuban, with the right of the dominion of the Euxine, and to the passage of the Dardanelles, was conceded to Russia.

New usurpations followed immediately on the part of the latter." As can be seen, the annexation of Crimea and Kuban happened only 5 years before American Admiral came to Russia. The quote above also provides a vivid illustration of how truly "historically Russian" Crimea was in view of the claims Moscow makes nowadays. The last sentence of the quote is also a perfect example of Russia's constant Modus Operandi – the signed treaty is just a new incentive for the new usurpations.

"In 1786, Catharine projected magnificent progress to the Euxine (Black Sea), where, after having solemnly taken the scepter of the Khan, it was her intention to conduct her young grandson, Constantine, to the gates of that city, with reference to whose contemplated destiny he had been named." It is quite interesting to learn that Empress Catherine named her grandson Constantine because she wanted to see him rule Constantinople, is it not?

The book also describes how Russia provoked Turkey to the point that the latter had to declare the war on it in the summer of 1787: "Eighty thousand men were ordered to march to cover Oczakow. A large army advanced to the Danube; and a squadron of 16 ships of the line, 8 frigates, and several gallies entered the Euxine under the command of the capitan-pacha. The Greeks were disarmed, and the Tartars invited to return to their allegiance to the grand seignior. They complied with the call, and their Shah had soon under his orders an army of 40,000 men. This news was received with joy at St. Petersburgh." Another trait of Moscow policy is to provoke as much as possible and try to play the role of a victim of aggression to the end.

John Paul Jones writes in his letter that on the 20th December 1787: "Mr. Jefferson, the ambassador of the United States, visited me on the night of my arrival, and informed me that M. de Simolin, minister plenipotentiary of her imperial majesty of all the Russians, … appeared anxious to succeed in prevailing on me to go to Russia, to command the fleet against the Turks in the Black Sea."

On 25 April 1788 John Paul Jones had his first audience with the Russian empress in St. Petersburg.

On the 19th May, he already met Potemkin at St. Elizabeth (city of Kropivnitsky in current day Ukraine), who "received me with much kindness, and destined me the command of the fleet of Sevastopol against the capitan-pacha, who, he supposed, intended to make descents in the Crimea. His highness was mistaken in this, and the next day he received information that the capitan pacha was at anchor within Kinbourn, having come to succor Oczakow with a hundred and twenty armed vessels and other armed craft. The prince marshal then, requested me to assume command of the naval force stationed in the Liman, (which is at the embouchure of the Dnieper,) to act against the capitan pacha till Oczakow should fall. I considered this change as a mark of confidence flattering to myself... having received my orders, I set out on the same day for Kherson, in company with the Chevalier de Ribas, Brigadier du Jour of the prince marshal."

According to his own testimony, initially John Paul Jones was to go to the Crimean port of Sevastopol, but the situation developed so quick, that he hoisted his flag on board the Wolodimir, a 70-cannon ship, already on the 26th of May, 1788, near the Ukrainian city of Kherson. The other two fortresses he mentions, are also on Ukrainian Black Sea shore not far away from the Dnieper embouchure.

It is hard to believe, but on top of all that, General Suvorov, commandant of Kinbourn, made the rear admiral responsible for the safety of that key fortress. There is even a note dated 31th of May from Suvorov to Jones where Suvorov declares that he cannot answer for results.

It means that already on the fifth day of his presence on the war theatre, Admiral Jones had full responsibility not just over the Russians Black Sea fleet, but also for the key fortress in their defense.

The American admiral writes that he was literally struck at finding the tongue of land at Kinbourn, which commanded the only passage by which large vessels could enter or come out of the Liman, without any artillery. He instantly spoke of it to Suvorov and proposed to establish one or more strong batteries upon it, which was done in a short while.

The squadron under Jones consisted of only one frigate carrying 40 guns of different calibers, four carrying 26, two 24, one 20, and one 16, and four vessels carrying in all 66 guns. His own vessel, the Wolodimir, a 70-gun ship, carried only 24 twenty-four pounders and two licornes - "the shallowness of the Liman would not allow of a greater weight of metal." It was significantly inferior to the Turkish fleet in almost everything.

There was only one force under his command though, John Paul Jones was truly impressed with: "Our force in rowboats is greatly superior to the Turks, and we can at any time go to the assistance of Kinbourn, though the wind should be contrary." Those rowboats were the famous Zaporozhian Cossack's chaikas, and, according to the Admiral's quote above, they were his major hope for maneuvering the large ships in case of even the contrary wind. It is worth mentioning also that several years before the war with Turkey, Catherine II ruined the Zaporozh Sich, but some Cossack troops still decided to fight on the Russian side.

During smaller battles during his first two weeks on the Black Sea, John Paul Jones had several occasions to demonstrate his typical derring-do: for example, in one of the most famous episode he approached at night a Turkish ship on a Cossack boat and painted "To be burnt. Paul Jones" on the ship's side, which was accomplished the next day.

The Cossacks were so impressed with his bravery, that on June 15, they awarded Jones the rare privilege of being inducted into the Cossack Brotherhood. Admiral was given a Cossack's smoking pipe, a sabre, and the red Cossacks trousers – sharovary, – which he proudly wore aboard his ship. During the ritual, he was also given a new Cossack name – Cossack Pavel Dzhones.

That is how the founder of the American Navy became an Honorary Cossack of the Zaporozhian Army.

By the 16th of June, the capitan pacha advanced with his whole fleet to attack.

"The rear admiral summoned a council of war to consult on what should be done. He addressed the council, at which were present all the commanders of the squadron and the flotilla, and concluded by telling them, ' that they must make up their minds to conquer or die for their country."

That is how one of the most crucial and famous Battle of the Liman started in John Paul Jones' own words: "The wind, which was rather fresh, being against us; the only thing proposed by the rear admiral that was found practicable was, to draw up our force in an obtuse angle, by bringing forward, by anchors, the right of the line up to the center. This movement was completed before midnight. The wind had shifted to N. N. E. and at break of day on the 17th, the rear admiral made a signal, and the whole squadron immediately set sail to commence the attack on the Turks. The Turks got into confusion the instant this maneuver was perceived. They raised their anchors or cut their cables with the greatest precipitation, and not the shadow of order remained in their fleet."

The major striking force under the circumstances became the above mentioned Ukrainian Zaporozhian Cossacks on their rowboats under the command of the two courageous atamans – Antin Holowaty, Sydir Bilyi and Zakhariy Chepega. During the Battle of June 17, the Cossacks fought so well, that John Paul Jones mentions some instances in his memoirs: "Some days afterwards, a colonel of Cossacks boarded the vessel run down in the road, and set fire to it, by leaving in it lighted brandcouglesi for which he received public thanks," and "the

Turkish fleet was now distant. The prince of Nassau was told that the Admiral's flag, which had been displayed on the vessel of the capitan pacha, was struck, and he hastily advanced to claim it... The Zaporozhians picked up the flag from the water, and the prince of Nassau, a long while afterwards, had the glory ...of having snatched it from their hands.

The battle turned as a great victory for John Paul Jones and his fleet. Even the battery he had installed on the tongue of land brought instant success: " At 10 o'clock on the night between the 17th and 18th of June, the capitan pacha attempted to carry the remains of his squadron, which had been defeated at eve, out of the Liman; but the block fort and battery fired on his ships, of which nine of the largest were forced aground upon the sandbank"

The victory came at a cost for the Ukrainian Cossacks -in the course of the battle, the Cossack ataman Sydir Bilyi was fatally wounded. General Potemkin wrote to Catherine of the accident, of the victory in which the major Turkish forces were defeated, and of the crucial role the Cossacks played in the Battle: "the Zaporozhians were of great service: if not for them, not our single ship would have been able to move."

In her reply, Catherine asked Potemkin to avoid using the word "Zaporozhians" to her. She asked to rename them into the *Black Sea Cossacks*. When the war was over, Catherine ordered to resettle the Cossacks to the Kuban, a territory near Caucus. It is where the other end of the present day notorious Kerch Bridge is. That was Catherine's gratitude for the Cossacks – to be deported from their Homeland to an unknown place where they were given some relative freedoms for a while.

Here is what a famous English traveler of the 19th century Dr. Edward Clark wrote in his book *Travels in Russia* some 12 years later on encountering those Cossacks: "The Tchernomorski (Black See

Cossacks) are a brave, but rude and warlike people, possessing little of the refinement of civilized society, although much inward goodness of heart; and they are ready to show the greatest hospitality to strangers who solicit their aid. Their original appellation was Zaporozhtzsi… In consequence of the service they rendered to Russia in her last war with Turkey, Catherine, by a ukase of the 2d of June 1792, ceded to them the peninsula of Taman, and all the countries between the Kuban and the Sea of Azof, as far as the rivers Ae and Laba ; an extent of territory comprehending upwards of 1000 square miles. They were allowed the privilege of choosing an ataman, but their numbers have considerably diminished. They could once bring into the field an army of 40,000 effective cavalry. At present, the number of troops which they are able to supply does not exceed 15,000."

How gracious was it for Catherine to take the homeland of the Zaporozhians and "cede" them the land recently taken from other nations and tribes! Not a bad choice of words for "deportation", is it?

Above is the monument in Krasnodar, city in Kuban region, Russia where the Black Sea Cossack were deported to and the city they founded. The first one in the picture is Grigory Potemkin, and then – the three Cossack atamans who fought shoulder to shoulder with John Paul Jones – Antin Holowatyi, Sydir Bilyi, Zakhariy Chepega. On top of the monument – Catherine. No mention of the American Admiral who might have saved Russia from the shameful defeat and masterminded a great victory instead.

"The distinctive mark of a Black Sea Cossack, borne by the lower order among them, of a braided lock from the crown of the head, passing behind the right ear, is retained even by the officers, but concealed by the younger part of them, with very artful foppery, among their dark hair. They seemed ashamed to have it noticed, although, like a relic on the breast of a Catholic, it was preserved even with religious veneration; and there was not one of them who would not sooner have parted with his life, than with this badge of the tribe to which he belonged," described Dr. Clark the "hohols."

What about John Paul Jones? A couple of months later having won several more sea battles, he had to leave his service because of the intrigues of Nassau and Potemkin.

By the time he had made his opinion of the naval capabilities of the Russians: ""It is surprising that the Russian seamen and pilots could be so profoundly ignorant respecting the anchorage, currents, and depth of the Liman, and, above all, at the entrance into the canal, (Fahz-water,) and in the road between Oczakow and Beresane. At first, not a single commander in the flotilla durst venture to cast an anchor."

One can easily sense bitterness in his passage: "For myself I have been marked among all the officers that served in the Liman, being the only one who obtained no promotion, though I commanded and was alone responsible!"

And the publisher of his memoirs adds the summary: "If he sometimes speaks in terms of bitterness of those with whom he acted,

40

it will be found that he had but too much cause to complain of them. He was treated with caprice; his due honors were sought to be wrested from him; he was sent back from the fleet cavalierly, and he was foully slandered. Over all this he triumphed in the issue completely, but his health and spirits were irretrievably affected by the ignoble and ungenerous persecution."

As the history shows, American Admiral and Ukrainian Cossacks turned out to be not just brothers in arms, but also brothers in misfortune of risking their lives for Russia.

Memorial to Admiral John Paul Jones in Kherson region, Ukraine

Admiral John Paul Jones died at the age of 45 in Paris during the French Revolution. He was buried in a lead coffin provided by his French friends at a cemetery, which was a part of the French royal family. Sometime later, the property was sold and the cemetery was forgotten.

When over a century later a search began to find the body of John Paul Jones to return his remains to the United States, there was a new town built on the property and over the cemetery. It took weeks of research and then tunneling through the streets and basements to locate the casket.

Inside the tightly sealed lead casket, the team discovered nearly perfectly preserved body wrapped up in a winding cloth and placed in straw and alcohol. The forensic study conducted at the University of Paris proved that it was John Paul Jones.

There were an impressive parade and a religious service in Paris first. Then a special squadron sent by Theodore Roosevelt brought John Paul Jones to Annapolis on July 24, 1905.

The casket of John Paul Jones was placed in the Academy's Hall to await completion of his permanent tomb.

Jones was bid to rest in the crypt of the Naval Academy Chapel on January 26, 1913. It is the 21-ton sarcophagus and surrounding columns of black and white Royal Pyrenees marble.

Point of Interest

To the lands of the Zaporozhian Cossacks, Catherine II lured the Mennonite believers from Prussia who started arriving already in 1789. The privileges promised included guarantees of religious freedom, exemption from military service and free land. 85 years later, on the eve of the new war with Turkey in 1874, Russia declared an intention to draft Mennonites into the army service. Not to take their chances, 900 Mennonite families immigrated to Canada and the USA. Among those families, there was a Groening family. Their grandson Homer born in Saskatchewan, during his childhood years could speak only the Plautdietsch dialect the settlers developed in Ukraine. Homer's son Matt, born in 1954, did not learn the dialect, but turned out to be very good at comics and cartoons.

4. Traveler Dr. Clark: "Superiority of Malo-Russians"

"We met frequent caravans of the Malo-Russians, who differ altogether from the inhabitants of the rest of Russia. Their features are those of the Polonese or Cossacks. They are a much more noble race, and stouter and better-looking people than the Russians, and superior to them in everything that can exalt one set of men above another. They are cleaner, more industrious, more honest, more generous, more polite, more courageous, more hospitable, more truly pious, and of course less superstitious... They have in many instances converted the desolate steppe into fields of corn. Their caravans are drawn by oxen, which proceed about thirty versts in a day. We began to perceive that the farther we advanced from the common hordes of the Russians, the more politeness and hospitality we should experience; exactly the reverse of that which we had been taught to expect by the inhabitants of Moscow."

This is a quote from the same book by Dr. Edward Clark mentioned in the previous chapter – *Travels in Russia, Tartary, and Turkey*. Preface to the 5th edition of it states: "Few works of travels have been more successful in gaining public approbation than those of Dr. Clarke. After an interval of twenty-eight years, the *Travels* of Dr. Clarke continue to maintain their place in public estimation." In other words and in modern terms, the passages already mentioned in this and the previous chapter, are from a bestseller of the 19th century Britain, written by arguably the most popular travel blogger of the time. And one of the most educated as well.

It is worth mentioning that for Dr. Clark, the Malo-Russians were the Ukrainians living to the east of the Dnieper river: "Concerning the inhabitants of the country called Malo-Russia, a French gentleman, who had long resided among them, assured me he used neither locks to his doors nor to his coffers; and among the Cossacks, as in Sweden, a trunk may be sent open, for a distance of 500 miles, without risking the loss of any of its contents."

The west, "right" bank of the Dnieper, he considered a part of former Poland annexed by Russia, - he even spells the name of Kiev in Polish manner – Kijov when writing about how Russia, Austria, and Prussia divided the "ancient republic of Poland." So, when Dr. Clark writes that by some information, the Don Cossacks originated in Poland, in reality, he refers to the territory of the Right-bank Ukraine.

Still being in the Russian city of Voronezh, Dr. Clark gets the feeling, that "the Russian finds it dangerous to travel in the Ukraine, and along the Don, because he is conscious that the inhabitants of these countries know too well with whom they have to deal," which tells a lot about reputation "the Russian" had among Ukrainians and the Don Cossacks. Approaching the borders of the present day eastern Ukraine and Russia's Rostov region, he makes another observation: "We began to perceive that the farther we advanced from the common hordes of the Russians, the more politeness and hospitality we should experience; exactly the reverse of that which we had been taught to expect by the inhabitants of Moscow."

It is interesting to see that just some 200 years ago, according to Dr. Clark descriptions, the Don Cossacks not just did not associate themselves with the Russians, but made every effort to avoid them. Why? "The Cossacks are justified in acting towards the Russians as they have uniformly done; that is to say, in withdrawing as much as possible from all communion with a race of men, whose association might corrupt, but could never advance, the interests of their society."

"We proceeded from Paulovskoy to Kazinskoy Chutor, a village inhabited by Malo-Russians and Russians mingled together. The distinction between the two people might be made without the smallest inquiry, from the striking contrast between filth and cleanliness…The first regular establishment of Malo-Russians which we saw, occurred after leaving Iestakovo. It was called Locova Sloboda. The houses were all whitewashed, like many of the cottages in Wales; and this operation is performed annually, with great care. Such distinguishing cleanliness appeared within them, that a traveler might fancy himself transported, in the course of a few miles, from Russia to Holland. Their apartments, even the ceilings, and the beams in the roof are regularly washed. Their tables and benches shine with washing and rubbing and reminded us of the interior of cottages in Norway. Their courtyard, stables, and out-houses, with everything belonging to them, bespoke industry and neatness. In their little kitchens, instead of the darkness and smoky hue of the Russians, even the mouths of their stoves were white. Their utensils and domestic vessels were all bright and well polished. They kept poultry and had plenty of cattle. Their little gardens were filled with fruit-trees, which gave an English character to their houses the third nation with whose dwellings I have compared the cottages of Malo-Russia; that is to say, having a Welsh exterior, a Norwegian interior, and the gardens and out-houses of the English peasantry."

A house of a poor superintendent villager so impressed the English travelers that Dr. Clark wrote that he would rather have dined on the floor of that apartment than "on the table of any Russian prince."

If Dr. Edward Clark associated Ukrainians with the English and Scandinavians, whom did he associate the Russians with?

"Until his time, however, Tartars were lords of Moscow the tsars themselves being obliged to stand in the presence of their ambassadors, while the latter sat at meat, and to endure the most humiliating ceremonies. Basilovich shook off the Tartar yoke; but it was a long time before the Russians, always children of imitation, ceased to mimic a people by whom they had been conquered. They had neither arts nor opinions of their own: everything in Moscow was Tartarian: dress, manners, buildings, equipages, in short, all except religion and language."

In Dr. Clark's opinion, even "the Kremle is derived from the Tartar word Tcrim, or krem, which signifies a fortress. It is situated on the north side of the Moskva, which flows below it, and it is triangular in form."

"They are all, high and low, rich and poor, alike servile to superiors; haughty and cruel to their dependents; ignorant, superstitious, cunning, brutal, barbarous, dirty, mean. The emperor canes the first of his grandees; princes and nobles cane their slaves; and the slaves their wives and daughters."

Point to stress

"Since the unsuccessful revolution of 1830, the aspect of affairs has been entirely changed. Poland has been treated as a conquered province, and its nationality utterly annihilated.

The Emperor Nicholas declared, by a ukase, that Poland had ceased to exist as a kingdom, and "that its inhabitants form but one nation with Russians, bound together by uniform and national sentiments." The diet was abolished, the Russian language substituted for the Polish in the tribunals, the University of Warsaw was closed, with the exception of the medical, theological, and astronomical classes, and its valuable collections of books, manuscripts, and medals, were carried off to Petersburg."

This is the way Russia treated all the countries and nations it invaded or occupied – Poland, Ukraine, Baltic states and others. If the term "Vempire" seemed a bit far-fetched for the reader, here is how Dr. Edward Clark saw Russia:

"Russia, morally considered, is like an enormous toad, extending on every side her bloated unwieldy form and gradually becoming weaker, as she swells with an unwholesome and unnatural expansion."

5. Napoleon on Russia. Ukrainian Lady-Warrior

In his recently published profound work *The First Scientific History of War of 1812*, contemporary Russian historian Evgenii Ponasenkov among other hundreds of documents quoted, gives account on Napoleon's own words on his conclusion of Russia. It can be found on pp. 612 – 614 of the book.

According to the writer, Napoleon did not expect and did not plan any war on Russia in 1812, because five years before that, after a series of victories over Russian troops and their allies, he was generous enough to sign the Treaties of Tilsit in 1807 with the Russian Tsar Alexander I. But the revengeful Russian tsar started preparing for a new war with Napoleon almost immediately and in 1811 already had armies standing on the border ready to invade Europe.

Then Alexander sent an ultimatum for Napoleon to move the French troops from the line along the Oder River, leaving Napoleon with no other option but to respond.

Napoleon wanted a fair battle on the border, but the Russian troops started a chaotic retreat using the tactics of "scorched land" burning their own cities and villages to the ground.

It is only in the vicinity of Moscow Kutuzov decided to finally give battle.

September 1, 1812, Napoleon writes to his Foreign Minister that in several days he is going to have a general battle and if he wins, he will capture Moscow.

In 6 days the Russians lost the battle and gave up Moscow.

In the 19th Bulletin of the Great Army, Napoleon informs the world about entering the city and discovering something terrible: "30 000 wounded Russian soldiers are in hospitals without medicines and food."

In the 20th Bulletin, Napoleon depicts the result of the hideous crime of Moscow mayor Rostopchin who ordered to set Moscow on fire: "30 000 of Russian wounded and sick burnt in the fire."

In the 21st Bulletin, Napoleon states: "The fire of this capital threw the country 100 years back."

The Kremlin was saved from fire by the French soldiers as a matter of fact.

From proclamation to the French Army May 03, 1813 after Napoleon had defeated the Russian Army again: "The Lutzen battle is in line with the battles like Austerlitz, Jena, Freedland, and Moscow-River. During the course of the previous campaign, the enemy did not think necessary to fight our armies to give up the savage methods used by its ancestors: armies of Tatars burnt their comrades, their own cities, their Holy Moscow. May they remain in their icy deserts, remain in slavery, in barbarism, in their corruption where a man is reduced to an animal!"

During his conversations with his companions already on the island of St Helena, Napoleon expressed his opinion on the reforms of Peter I: "He (Peter) did not want to leave the Russians as Asians," but with no success. "The Russians are barbarians who do not have a sense of their Homeland." "Russians are poor and it creates for them the necessity of conquest, moving elsewhere."

Tatars, savage methods, barbarism, slaves, Asians who burn their own cities and comrades alive– that is how Napoleon viewed Russians.

A couple of words about "Russian Tsar" Alexander I. He was tsar of Russia, but he was not Russian altogether. He belonged to the same

Holstein-Gottorp Prussian (German) dynasty just as his grandmother Catherine II. "Romanov dynasty" was more like a cover-up name for them. The rule of this dynasty in Russia will end when the Bolsheviks kill the whole family of Nikolai II after the October "Revolution" in 1917.

Unfortunately, German tsar of Russia Alexander I and his "Tatars" affected the destiny of Napoleon in many senses – Napoleon would have accomplished much more but for the wars with Russia.

"One day Europe will realize how prudent my Russian campaign was," - wrote Napoleon on February 14, 1817. "Europe does not have much time, neither have I. Misfortune of barbarians inflow will become a revenge for rejecting my policy."

What was Ukraine's attitude toward Napoleon's war on Russia? Whose side Ukraine supported?

In the same book mentioned above, on p. 157, the author cites a unique document which illustrates not just the attitude, but the spiritual power of Ukrainian women we are going to witness again in the later chapters of this book.

Lithuanian Courier # 58, 1812

An offer of a LADY-WARRIOR

Message from Warsaw, July 26, 1812

Two days ago young and beautiful Ukrainian lady, dressed in uhlan uniform which befitted her well, came to Duke Czartoryski and announced that her last name is Nachvasky which is well known in Ukraine.

Then she said that she came from the city of Zhitomir, her husband serves in the Polish Army for a long time already and she loves her Homeland no less than he does and hates Russians no less as well, and that is why she strives to share all the dangers and happiness with him.

As soon as she learned of the military actions beginning, she let her lady-friends know of her intentions, and at once 200 of them expressed desire to serve their Homeland together with her, but in the beginning, she decided to take only those, who had the desire as strong as her own. As a result, she joined with 15 women for whom she vouches as for herself.

Marshall applauded admiring her courage but assuming she came to him to ask for uniforms arming for her squad, said that he will try to render a feasible help.

To that the beautiful Ukrainian replied that her estate and fortune, as well as the fortunes of her lady-friends, are sufficient to cover all the expenses; all they need is the arms and horses and that is why she decided to come to Warsaw. After that, she added that in several days she with her group are going to the Army."

ROXELANA

In the year 1520, a young Ruthenian/Rusian/Ukrainian girl was taken into captivity not far away from Lviv. Most likely via the Kaffa slave market, she was sold into the imperial harem in Istanbul. Her name was Aleksandra Lisowska and she had something so special in her character, that the Ottoman Sultan broke several rules and traditions of the time and took her as his official wife. As the "Queen of Ottoman Empire," Roxelana played an active role in state affairs and became one of the most influential women in the history of the country. She had 5 children securing the future of the Ottoman dynasty. There is a Mausoleum with her body in Istanbul and a monument in her hometown in Ukraine.

6. WWI, Two Independent Ukraines, Wilsonian hope

The same years Catherine II of Russia was capturing what would be known in present times as Belarus, Austria seized some lands of the Polish-Lithuanian Commonwealth for itself.

The territory it partitioned in 1772 and 1795 was home to more than two million East Slavic peasants and had very fertile land.

It became a crownland of the Habsburg monarchy known as "Galicia and Lodomeria," where "Lodomeria" was a Latinized name for Volhynia and was derived from a town whose eponymous founder was Kiev King Vladimir the Great. He was the one who founded it and incorporated it into Kiev Rus in 981.

"Galicia" was a name given by the Habsburg dynasty after the medieval principality of Halych. One of the theories states that "Halych" derives from the Slavic word "halka", "jackdaw" in English. Jackdaw featured on the coat of arms of the Kingdom of Galicia and Lodomeria is a sign that the theory is true.

Eastern Galicia was also called Red Ruthenia, or Red Rus. It was mostly situated on the upper Dniester River.

The full ceremonial name of that entity actually was The Kingdom of Galicia and Lodomeria and the Grand Duchy of Krakow with the Duchies of Auschwitz and Zator.

Yes, the Auschwitz.

During the first decades of Austrian rule, Galicia was governed from Vienna. But later on, the Kingdom was mostly under control of the Polish landholders.

Poles were the majority in the western part of the province, with Krakow being the largest city after 1846.

Ukrainians (Rusians, Ruthenians) were the majority in the eastern part, where Lviv was the largest city.

Lviv, also called Lemberg, became the capital of Austrian Galicia and started growing fast - in a little more than a 100 years period of time it grew sevenfold - from 20 thousand to roughly 140 thousand.

Apart from Ukrainians and Poles, there was a strong Jewish community.

The Jews of Galicia had come in the Middle Ages from Germany and mostly spoke Yiddish as their first language. German-speaking people were more commonly referred to by the region of Germany where they originated (e.g. Saxons or Swabians).

The city was becoming an intellectual center of the time and gave the world several bright personalities:

Paul Muni (Weisenfreund) - one of Hollywood's finest character actors, "second Lon Chaney", "the man with a thousand faces."

Weegee (Arthur Fellig), famous New York photographer of the 1940s was born and spent his childhood in Lviv.

Hedy Lamarr's father, Emil Kiesler, was born and became a successful bank director in it.

Simon Wiesenthal - founder and head of the Jewish Documentation Center, a longtime Nazi hunter. (Golda Meir was born as Golda Mabovitch and spent her childhood in Kiev, Vladimir Horowitz too; Sholem Aleichem – near Kiev)

Leopold Sacher-Masoch – the one who invented the literary character of the Masochist in the 1870s.

Here is a monument to him in the city of Lviv.

Adam Bruno Ulam - one of the world's foremost authorities on the Soviet Union. Member of the Harvard faculty from 1947 where Robert Kennedy and Henry Kissinger were among his students.

Great Ukrainian historian Mykhailo Hrushevs'kyi - taught in Lviv in the Ukrainian language starting 1895. His "History of Ukraine-Rus'" book became the most important text in the construction of a Ukrainian historical narrative. In that work, Hrushevs'ky refuted Russian claim to Ukraine.

Currently, two World Chess Champions in blitz and quick chess Anna Muzychuk and Vasily Ivanchuk live in Lviv.

By the way, the Kerosene lamp was also invented in Lviv. Here is a tourist attraction devoted to the event:

Before WWI, Lviv and Eastern part of Galicia were ready and demanded a Ukrainian autonomy together with proportional representation in the Galician and Austrian parliaments. As well as Ukrainization of Lviv University. The long-term goal was also the establishment of a Ukrainian State according to the ethnic borders.

During the First World War, in which Austria fought Russia, Ukrainian cause had its obvious chance. Galician Ukrainian politicians who were present in Vienna aided the cause any possible way they could - they clearly realized that it was a unique chance to establish an Independent Ukraine not just in Galicia, but on all ethnic Ukrainian lands freed from Russia.

As a result, West Ukrainian Republic was established November 9, 1918, by the Ukrainian National Rada in Lviv.

After the February Revolution in Russia, and the proclamation of the Ukrainian National Republic in Kyiv in early 1917, some bright spots hinting at independence appeared.

After the American entry into the war in April 1917, Galician Ukrainians were encouraged by the rhetoric of Wilsonian self-determination, because it basically provided the same opportunity to become independent no matter who won the war.

On December 1, 1918, the State Secretariat of the Western Ukrainian National Republic concluded a preliminary agreement with the Directory of the Ukrainian National Republic on the union of the two Ukrainian States. The agreement was approved by the Ukrainian National Rada in Kiev on January 3, 1919, and by the Directory on January 22. The Union was proclaimed in a special proclamation on January 22.

But...

After Denikin's defeat, the Western powers made a decision to support Poland as a counterweight to Bolshevik Russia, and Poland used this support to claim eastern Galicia and Lviv.

The two Ukrainian states founded after the WWI, with capitals in Lviv and Kiev, now had little chance for independence.

The first time Kiev was overtaken by the Muraviov army sent by Trotsky in February of 1918. Many historic buildings were demolished by artillery on purpose after the city had already quit resisting. The city was looted for two weeks and many civilians, including women, were executed for no reason. Approximately 1 000 officers and generals were shot.

The Bolsheviks invaded Ukraine in late December of the same year. On January 16, 1919, Ukraine officially declared war on Russia while the Russian Soviet government continued to deny all claims of invasion. (The same dirty trick of non-recognition of invasion Russia

55

will be using over and over again including the recent hybrid war on Ukraine in Donbas and earlier Crimea annexation).

By June 1919, Polish forces occupied eastern Galicia succeeding in driving the West Ukrainian Republic's Army of the eastern Galicia.

After that, Poland tried to get Entente recognition for its claims on the whole Galicia.

Initially, the Supreme Council of the Paris Peace Conference representing the Entente instructed Poland to occupy Ukrainian Galicia temporarily, thus recognizing Galicia's special status.

On November 20, it drafted a treaty with Poland on the autonomy of eastern Galicia under the higher administration of Poland for 25 years, but the Poles rejected the draft.

The Conference of Ambassadors of the Entente finally recognized the Polish occupation, albeit with the provision that eastern Galicia was to remain autonomous.

Despite the provision, Poles quickly established their administrations and started treating the region as a part of Poland.

The war cost Galician Ukrainians close to 20,000 in casualties and intensified the hard feelings of Ukrainians toward Poland.

The west Ukrainian Republic was forced to establish a government-in-exile in Vienna.

There could have been, in some sense, a United States of Ukraine.

Many participants of those events, Entente included, will be wishing it would have happened.

Point of Interest

Kuban People's Republic declared independence on February 16, 1918. It included the territory between the Sea of Azov and the

Caspian Sea where the Black Sea Cossacks were resettled to under conditions described in a previous chapter.

Almost immediately, the new Republic declared its intent to form a union with the Ukrainian People's Republic.

Kuban People's Republic lasted only for 21 months and was crushed by the Bolsheviks in November 1919.

In April 1918, Ukrainian People's Republic forces under command of Col. Petro Bolbochan entered Crimea and seized Sevastopol and the Black Sea Fleet.

Later, under German pressure, however, the Ukrainian troops had to withdraw from Crimea, the ships first came under German, and then under the Allied control who later gave them to the White Russians.

With Kuban and Crimea – that is how Ukraine looked in 1919.

Мапа України, що представлена на Паризькій мирній конференції 1919 року.
(відповідно до умов Брестського мирного договору 1918 року).
Map of Ukraine from the Paris Peace Conference in 1919.
(according to the Treaty of Brest-Litovsk signed in 1918).

7. Mennonite Botanist

Do you recall the Mennonite community briefly mentioned at the end of the chapter about Admiral John Paul Jones? Here is a story written in the first person.

"I was born in the city of Yekaterinoslav (March 4, 1898) (Ekaterinoslav; to be referred to further as E.), now called Dnepropetrovsk. The city was originally named after the Zarin Katherine the Great who promoted agriculture in the steppes of the Ukraine by inviting settlers from Germany, among them the Mennonites. My family are Mennonites. Our family on the Esau side dates back to my great-grandfather Aron Esau, who immigrated in 1804 from Prussia.

In the fall of 1916, I entered the Golitsin Women's Agricultural College in Moscow, starting with natural sciences, physics, chemistry, and geology.

Perhaps I should mention here why I chose agricultural sciences. It was not a well-considered plan. I liked working with plants, and agriculture appeared to deal with them in a more interesting way than botany, which seemed to be mainly naming plants.

…The Revolution interrupted our schooling after the first year, at the end of 2 semesters (1916-1917). Travel became impossible and I remained in E. waiting for further developments.

…The war came close to home when the German army advanced and succeeded in occupying the Ukraine.

…The German army continued to move east. Their advance prevented the Bolsheviks from spreading, especially in the Ukraine, because they wanted the Ukraine separate from Russia and incorporated with Germany. So they came fully equipped for war, if necessary. We were very comfortable because they didn't touch the local population... Of course, the Germans were very anxious to make a good impression on the people because they realized that in order to successfully annex the captured territory; they had better be on good terms with the local population

...When the war ended, the German officers warned that the population would be in great danger after the army left and advised us to flee with them to Germany. We and many other people followed this advice and our family of four departed.

...My first thought, after arriving in Germany, was that I should find a school where I would want to study. I think they were just beginning the spring semester. I had my Russian documents with me and I went to an agricultural school."

These were the excerpts from *Autography* by Katherine Esau.

After completing the Agricultural College of Berlin, the Esau family moved to a Mennonite community in Reedley, California, where Katherine resumed her education at the University of California. She achieved her doctorate in 1931.

Her *Plant Anatomy*, known worldwide as the bible of plant anatomy, was published in 1953. *Anatomy of Seed Plants* saw the light in 1960.

In 1989, President George Bush awarded Esau the National Medal of Science.

8. An Undefeated Ukrainian Wrestler & the USA Male Beauty Contest

Please meet a man whose name Russia uses as a symbol of "Russian power" - Ivan Poddubny.

But was he really "Russian"?

As we consult any open source, we read that Ivan Poddubny was born in 1871 into a family of Zaporozhian Cossacks in the village of Krasenivka, present-day Chornobai Region of Cherkasy Oblast, Ukraine. He had three younger brothers and three sisters, so it was a large Cossack family.

Who cares it was at the time under the rule of or occupied by the Russian Empire!

Why does it matter Ivan Poddubny lived at the time under the rule of or occupied by the Russian Empire!? The readers of the 2nd Chapter now have one extra example why Muscovy chose to become "Russia". As history has already established, Ivan Poddubny was of a Zaporozhian Cossacks' family. He was an heir of those fearless warriors who fought Muscovy -"Russia" - all their history.

His beautiful, typical Ukrainian last name actually has a meaning and can and must be translated as "the one under the oak". And what an "Oak" Ivan truly was!

He started his sports career when he was around 30 (in 1900) and ended wrestling when he was 70, losing only twice during his whole life.

His career began in a circus where he wore Cossack attire and performed different tricks with heavy weights. Simultaneously, he began wrestling.

He wrestled all over Europe in cities like Paris, Vienna, and Frankfurt where he fought primarily in the Greco-Roman style.

There is a story of Ivan losing one of those two wrestling matches to a cheating French champion, Raoul Le Boucher, who used oil to grease his skin and thus was much harder to subdue. The judges gave the victory to the French athlete for his "defenses". It angered Ivan so greatly that the next time he met Le Boucher in competition, Ivan subdued his opponent in half position and was spanking him for almost 20 minutes while at the same time explaining the rules of fair wrestling. Humiliated, Le Boucher hired assassins, but the plot was revealed, and Le Boucher was himself killed by the assassins he hired for refusing to pay for the work he considered not done.

In the 1920s, Poddubny came to the US on tour when he was already 50 years old. But truly, as if he were an oak, he appeared to have become stronger with age. The power he had can be described by the fact that the everyday walking stick he had custom made of steel weighed 16 kilograms (35 pounds). He used it consistently to keep his arms, wrists, and shoulders in shape.

He once confessed that the only person stronger than himself was his father.

During his tour, Ivan wrestled in cities like New York City, Los Angeles, Philadelphia, Chicago, San Francisco. He had to fight freestyle, within certain requirements, which was new to him, but he still won all the bouts.

Quite an unusual event happened to Ivan during that time - for some reason he decided to participate in a beauty, predecessor of Mr. Olympia, contest for men, which happened to take place nearby where he wrestled.

Despite being 56 years old, he won the contest.

If it was money that motivated him to participate, Poddubny surely was disappointed - he was unable to receive the half million dollars as a reward because he was not a citizen.

On his return home, he was arrested by NKVD (an earlier version of KGB) agents and put into prison where he was tortured. Among other things, the NKVD agents wanted to know of possible bank accounts abroad and how to receive the money.

One year later Ivan was released and continued his wrestling career.

He died in 1949 and was buried in a Russian city of Yesk.

At his grave, there was once an obelisk that said, "Here lies the Russian bogatyr (strongman)". However, in 1988 somebody destroyed the obelisk and wrote "Hohol-Petliuravite". It was an anti-Ukrainian slur, where "hohol" stands for the "forelock" Zaporozhian Cossacks wore, and "Petliurovite", meaning the follower of Simon Petliura, one of the fighters for Ukrainian Independence against Russian occupants and Bolsheviks.

What were the grounds for the Russians to call Ivan those names?

Below is a unique portrait painted during Ivan's visit home where he poses in typical Zaporozhian Cossack attire and with a forelock on his head. He is painted in his full height. It is quite an impressive portrait, and the painting is kept in one of Ukraine's museums.

In his autobiography, Ivan wrote that his lifelong personal motto were the words his father taught him:

"Cossack honor is above all else."

<u>Note of interest</u>. In aspect of Ivan Poddubny's legacy, it was a bit unexpected for Ukrainians when current Ukrainian wrestler, Fedor Emelianenko, who many viewed as an heir of Ivan Poddubny, decided to change his citizenship to Russian. Fedor Emelianenko was born in Ukraine, clearly possesses Ukrainian looks, and has a Ukrainian last name.

He may be wishing that he had not changed citizenship already since recently there were some bad words said in his address.

Not because of his ethnical background yet, although it may come one day also.

Just as a part of "Russian world" reality.

As for the physical might, Ukraine still has the true heirs of Ivan Poddubny.

Taiho, arguably the greatest Sumo wrestler of all time, was of Ukrainian descent and was called Ivan Boryshko at birth.

Already a governor of California, Arnold Schwarzenegger wrote to a Ukrainian weightlifter Leonid Zhabotinsky that he was actually his fan since his adolescence in Austria: "At the Mexico Olympiad I supported my countrymen, but worried a lot about you." Zhabotinsky received two Olympic Gold Medals and set 19 World Records between 1963 and 1974.

In 2004, another Ukrainian Vasyl Virastyuk became the Strongest Man on Earth.

Vitaly and Vladimir Klitschko are also not far from being called Ukrainian strongmen, with Vitaly becoming the first Ukrainian boxer elected to the International Boxing Hall of Fame.

Another Ukrainian boxer may be not so impressive in size as the Klitschko brothers, but is already setting records in getting the boxing titles – Vasyl "Hi-Tech" Lomachenko. There is a story, mentioned in an HBO pre-fight documentary, about his father enrolling 6-year old Vasyl in a Ukrainian Cossack dance group to train his legs agility to give his son advantage in the ring.

Sport Illustrated named Vasyl's father, Anatoliy Lomachenko, (the magazine nicknamed him "Papachenko"), the Boxing Trainer of the Year 2018.

And Forbes magazine put the undisputed 200-pound champion Oleksander Usyk as #1 on Future Boxing Moneymakers' List.

9. Kiev boy with Da Vinci dreams. US Presidents' helicopters

Leonardo da Vinci - was the name which entered the dreams of a little boy growing up in a luxurious building in central Kiev at the very beginning of the 20th century.

It was his mother's story about the genius of the fifteenth century who envisioned a flying machine that could take off in the air without acceleration using only something like rotating blades that impressed a young boy imagination.

Then the boy read Jules Verne's novel *Robur the Conqueror* and decided in his own mind he would become the engineer who would make it work in real life.

The boy's name was Igor Sikorsky.

The Sikorskys were well known in Kiev. Igor's father Ivan was a prominent psychiatrist, MD, and long-term Chairman of the St. Vladimir University in Kiev.

Igor Sikorsky's mother, Maria, was a highly educated woman but devoted her life to her family, which consisted of five children.

In 1900, Igor entered the First Kyiv Gymnasium, the oldest Kiev school with great educational traditions. The world famous writer Mikhail Bulgakov, among others, was also a graduate of the Gymnasium among others.

Since Igor's elder brother Sergei studied at the Sea Cadet Corps in St. Petersburg, his parents decided that the youngest son had to study there too.

Igor quickly realized that a naval military career was not what he really wanted, so he devoted more and more time to inventing different things in the workshops dreaming of the sky instead.

He was even more motivated after he read in the newspapers of the Wright brothers' flight.

A couple years later, he returned home and entered Kiev Polytechnic Institute (KPI) which was walking distance from his home.

At that time (1905-1906), the mechanical department of KPI organized the aeronautical workshop of airplanes, helicopters, engines, and ornithopters (a machine that flew by use of flapping wings).

The workshop turned out to become quite productive, and by 1909-1912 created about 40 different types of aircraft - more than had ever been created in the center of Russian aviation - St. Petersburg. Igor Sikorsky was one of the moving figures of the process.

In 1908, student Sikorsky began working on the design and construction of his first helicopter.

The process took place at his father's estate, and his father had to sponsor Igor's trip to France so Igor could take first flying lessons and buy an engine for his first helicopter.

Igor's first helicopter did not fly as well as his second, for which he returned to Paris for another engine. The technologies of that time simply were not ready for such the challenge of a helicopter.

Igor Sikorsky with his Helicopter #2 in 1910, Kiev,

The young designer switched to developing his first airplane, for which two hangars were built at the Institute and two more in the future flying field nearby.

The planes were the BIS-1 and BIS-2 (acronyms for Bylinkin, Iordan, and Sikorski who worked together), and the C-3, C-4, C-5 and C-6, on which Sikorsky worked basically alone.

It was on the C-6 that Sikorski set two world speed records of that time- two passengers flying at 111 kilometers per hour, and with five passengers – 106 kilometers per hour. Both records were set in Kiev.

Sikorsky preferred to fly his own airplanes by the way.

In April 1912, the plane C-6A was shown at an exhibition of aeronautics in Moscow and received the Grand Gold Medal.

With such an achievement, still a Kiev student, Igor Sikorsky was invited to work in St. Petersburg and became a chief designer of the air branch of a famous company of those days.

That position provided Igor Sikorsky with the means to increase capacity and improve the reliability and safety of his aircraft by installing multiple engines.

The final result of the work turned out to become the best aircraft of the time, the famous *Ilya Muromets*. The plane was named after a folk hero of Kiev Rus, a knight-errant buried in Kiev Cave Monastery.

To prove the skeptics wrong who claimed that such a heavy machine could not fly higher than one kilometer, Sikorsky personally flew the plane at 2 kilometers high, breaking the current at the time world record in altitude. After that he, together with three other crew members, broke another record flying from Petersburg to Kiev in June 1914. Several days later the plane made the trip back.

During the First World War, the C-22, which was the official name of the *Ilya Muromets*, had more than two dozen versions. It was the scariest bomber of that War as well.

WW1 ended with the Bolshevik Revolution in Russia and Igor Sikorsky decided to emigrate.

Initially, in March 1918, he moved to France, but in the war-exhausted country, it was not the time for aviation projects.

So Sikorski decided to move to the United States where the world famous engineer in his first year had to teach mathematics to Russian-speaking immigrants in New York.

As in Kiev 15 years earlier, there was again a group of enthusiasts and a little financial help from a composer - Sergei Rachmaninov - that provided the opportunity for Sikorsky to start aviation engineering again.

But it was in 1924 when the first aircraft was completed on American soil - the S-29A, "A" standing for "American". In 1927 the plane was sold to a popular businessman and pilot Roscoe Turner, who flew it frequently. Later the plane was purchased by a Hollywood film studio and appeared in a movie about the WW2 air battles.

Eventually, the company managed to buy land in Stratford, Connecticut, and built a modern Aircraft Manufacturing Factory.

All this time Sikorski simultaneously worked on developing his helicopter. So, when in 1938 the US Congress managed to allocate three million dollars to counter German achievement in helicopter building and build a helicopter for the US Army, Sikorsky was ready.

Unlike German transverse design, Sikorski stuck to his initial single-rotor scheme with a tail rotor, the one he invented in Kiev, and proved right – already in 1942 the U.S. Army accepted his VS-316.

Versions of this helicopter were used by the US and British troops till the end of WWII.

It was this helicopter that in extreme weather conditions, in 1944, for the first time in history, participated in saving sailors from the US destroyer *Turner,* hit by a German submarine.

There is a powerful documentary available on Youtube on how the S-70 Battlehawk Sikorsky helicopter was created and what it meant for the contemporary US Military.

In 1957, American President Dwight D. Eisenhower started using Sikorsky UH-34 Seahorse as his Marine One. Now the "White Tops" are either Sikorsky VH-3D Sea King or the smaller VH-60N White Hawk.

There were many other achievements of the Sikorsky Corporation, but the very fact that the Presidents of the most technologically advanced nation in the world still, sixty years later, choose to fly Sikorsky's machines, means that the company is still on the cutting edge of technological advances.

As for Igor Sikorsky's homeland, the building where he lived with his family is still there - very close to the Golden Gate built by Yaroslav the Wise and on the street that has the Great Kiev King's name - Yaroslaviv Val. The building needs repairs and the Kievans hope that one day there will be a museum of the father of helicopter industry.

The Kiev Polytechnic Institute now wears the Sikorsky name, and in 2015, on the premises of the institution, the current Mayor of Kiev, Vitaly Klitschko (yes, the Heavyweight Boxing Champion) and the Mayor of New York, Rudolf Guiliani, opened the first monument to the father of helicopter industry, Igor Sikorsky.

The monument includes some of Sikorsky's last words:

"Hats off to the alma mater, which prepared me to conquer the sky. »

We, on our part, say, "Hats off to a man who made one of Da Vinci's dreams come true and contributed to humankind so much."

Point of origin

The author of this book wants to confess that to himself he was almost confident that Igor Sikorsky must have been at least partially of Polish origin. Just like Kazimir Malevich who was also born in Kiev, but was of Polish descent.

And only recently the author came across a letter Igor Sikorsky wrote in English to Dr. Halich with the following passage in it:

"My family purely Ukrainian origin, from the village in the Kyiv region, where my great-grandfather and great-grandfather were priests"

This letter still exists and is stored in the Fund Galich in the archives of the University of Minnesota among Wasyl Halich, Ph.D. papers. Box 2. Folder 13.

Recently, Kiev mayor Vitaly Klitschko opened another monument to Igor Sikorsky. It is situated near the second-largest Kiev airport that was named after the prominent Ukrainian aviation engineer.

10.   "Flying Fortress" the K-7

It's hard not to mention another outstanding plane built in Ukraine at the time Sikorsky was building his planes already in the United States.

The Kalinin "Flying Fortress."

This sky-monster was designed to be either a heavy bomber or a civilian/troop plane capable of carrying up to 120 people.

The plane was basically one hollow wing 53 meters long with a wingspan of 53 meters. Its contemporary US heavy bomber Martin B-10 which had its first flight in 1932 had a wingspan of only 21.5m.

K-7 had seven engines, three on each side of the main wing and one at the rear.

Mistakenly, this scary looking plane was called the "Russian Flying Fortress".

First of all, the K-7 was designed and produced in Kharkiv which at the time was the capital of the Ukrainian Socialist Republic in the years between 1919 and 1934. (Kiev was constantly revolting against

Bolsheviks and it was dangerous place for communist authorities there all that period of time).

Another interesting detail is that the designer of the plane, Konstantin Kalinin studied at Kiev Polytechnic Institute just as Igor Sikorsky, but some 17 years later - in 1924.

Knowing this fact, it is safe to assume who affected the design of such a monster as K-7 because Sikorsky S-22 "Ilya Muromets", four-engine world record setter plane, landed in Kyiv just 10 years before Konstantin Kalinin entered Kiev Institute.

K-7 was assembled and flew its first flights also in the then-capital of Ukraine, city of Kharkiv.

It did show some weaknesses during the test flights, with vibrations being the major problem. Konstantin Kalinin was confident that it could be eliminated. But on its 8th flight in November 1933, the plane crashed.

Initially, it looked like the cause of the crash was the result of vibration, but there recently appeared speculations in the Russian aviation press that there was a sabotage from the competing Russian Tupolev design office at the time, which led to the crash of K-7. The crash killed 14 people on board and 1 on the ground.

If the speculations of the sabotage are true, then Russia did take part in the fate of the Flying Fortress indeed, but not in the way it was presented and believed worldwide.

One more thing to demonstrate Russia's "input" into the technical progress - 5 years after the K-7 crash, Konstantin Kalinin was executed in Russia as "enemy of the State".

Russia did everything to destroy Kalinin airplane and Kalinin himself, so it is not correct from this perspective also to call K-7 Flying Fortress "Russian".

It is yet another symbol of Ukrainian aspiration for the sky, which was shot on the fly.

Memory of Konstantin Kalinin is not lost.

And Ukrainian power and spirit of the K-7 Flying Fortress and Sikorski S-22 live on and abide nowadays in Antonov AN-225 "Mriya" which in Ukrainian means "Dream".

Below is the only monument to Konstantin Kalinin which is situated at Kiev Polytechnic Institute where he created his first plane, K-1, which would become the USSR's first passenger plane. To the left of Kalinin there is one of his last and most ambitious project – K-15, - the jet fighter with delta wings in 1938! The monument to Kalinin is right across from the one to Sikorsky. It is now known that Ihor Sikorsky urged Kalinin twice to come to the USA.

11.   Great Depression, Stalin's Grapes of Wrath for Ukraine - Holodomor

Black Tuesday, when the American stock market crashed happened October 29, 1929.

In just one week's time, November 7 during his speech devoted to the 12th anniversary of the Bolshevik Revolution, Stalin described the socialist alternative to the market - State planning for almost everything which was to bring stability and help avoid any unpredictable shocks.

For agricultural sector, it would mean that "old countryside" of household farmers will be replaced by collective farms. Proletariat needed a stable inflow of food in the cities to complete industrialization of the first socialist state in humankind history, Stalin declared.

Also, more grain was needed to sell abroad to buy technological equipment.

The major source of all the agricultural products for the USSR was "the breadbasket" Ukraine with the freedom-loving peasantry. Because of that, the policy of collectivization in Ukraine was collapsing - peasants massively were abandoning collective farms taking their property back with them: livestock, wheat, equipment.

The very thing that the capital of Ukraine still had to be in Kharkiv because Right-Bank Ukraine including Kiev was causing trouble, was getting on Moscow's nerves.

The Great Depression in the United States did not lead to the starvation in Ukraine of course, but it surely brought Moscow the false assurance that the chosen path to communism was correct. It also made Stalin regime more resolved in reaching its goal and as soon as possible.

Stability in the whole Soviet Union depended on appeasing of Ukrainian peasantry. It's either Moscow breaks the backbone of independent Ukrainian farmers, basically turning them into serfs at the collective farms, or there will be a Great Depression in the USSR and very soon.

So the "class warfare" policy in the countryside was announced and the troops were sent to encircle Ukrainian villages and to remove basically all food from the farmers.

The "Law of Spikelets" which foresaw 10 years imprisonment with confiscation of property or execution even for harvesting the crop leftovers was accepted August 7, 1932.

That date can be considered the starting point of Holodomor which is a combination of two words: "Holod", meaning hunger, and "Mor", extermination.

"Starvation was the result of the forcible removal of food from peoples' home; roadblocks that prevented peasants seeing work or food; blacklists imposed on farms and villages," writes an American historian Ann Applebaum in her book "Red Famine: Stalin's war on Ukraine."

Why not simply shoot, kill the farmers and take the food, some wonder? It looks like the major task was to create a population of agricultural slaves without any nationality but with the inborn sense of fear. "To starve into submission the rebellious Ukrainian peasantry" - would be the correct definition of what Stalin regime was trying to accomplish.

So, unlike the Joads from the John Steinbeck's acclaimed novel, Ukrainian farmers could not even relocate - they were encircled by the Russian troops. And the reason for their life-and-death situation was not the lack of food caused by the Dust Bowl. It was caused by the Bowl, or, even Cyclone which consisted of socialist utopian ideas which took hold in the minds of Ukraine's northern neighbor. It included Stalin's personal hatred toward Ukraine. But, most of all - Muscovy's obsessive desire to occupy and completely submit freedom-loving Ukraine.

In summer of 1933, at the height of the Holodomor, 28,000 men, women and children were dying of starvation each day in Ukraine.

The total number of deaths during Holodomor - no less than 3.5 million people but numbers up to 6 million appear more often.

On September 20, 1953, Prof. Raphael Lemkin, author of the United Nations Convention against Genocide described the Holodomor as one part of "perhaps the classic example of Soviet genocide, its longest and broadest experiment in Russification—the destruction of the Ukrainian nation."

In his opinion, the Russification started already during the previous centuries and was "only the logical successor of such Tsarist crimes as the drowning of 10,000 Crimean Tatars by order of Catherine the Great, the mass murders of Ivan the Terrible's 'SS troops' — the Oprichnina; the extermination of National Polish leaders and Ukrainian Catholics by Nicholas I; and the series of Jewish pogroms that have stained Russian history periodically. And it has had its matches within the Soviet Union in the annihilation of the Ingerian nation, the Don and Kuban Cossacks, the Crimean Tatar Republics, the Baltic Nations of Lithuania, Estonia and Latvia. Each is a case in the longterm policy of liquidation of non-Russian peoples by the removal of select parts."

"Ukrainian is not and has never been, a Russian. His culture, his temperament, his language, his religion — all are different. At the side door to Moscow, he has refused to be collectivized, accepting deportation, even death. And so it is peculiarly important that the Ukrainian be fitted into the Procrustean pattern of the ideal Soviet man."

In Dr. Lemkin's opinion, the Moscow offensive against Ukraine was four-pronged and systematic and was repeated over and over to meet fresh outbursts of national spirit.

The first blow was aimed at the intelligentsia, the national brain, so as to paralyze the rest of the body. "In 1920, 1926 and again in 1930–1933, teachers, writers, artists, thinkers, political leaders, were liquidated, imprisoned or deported."

The second blow was an offensive against the churches, priests and hierarchy, the 'soul' of Ukraine. "Between 1926 and 1932, the Ukrainian Orthodox Autocephalous Church, its Metropolitan Lypkivsky and 10,000 clergies were liquidated."

The third prong was aimed at the farmers, ''the repository of the tradition, folklore and music, the national language and literature, the national spirit, of Ukraine. The weapon used against this body is perhaps the most terrible of all — starvation. Between 1932 and 1933, 5,000,000 Ukrainians starved to death.

"The crop that year was ample to feed the people and livestock of Ukraine, though it had fallen off somewhat from the previous year, a decrease probably due in large measure to the struggle over collectivization.

As W. Henry Chamberlain, the Moscow correspondent of the /Christian Science Monitor/, wrote in 1933: The Communists saw in this apathy and discouragement, sabotage and counter-revolution, and, with the ruthlessness peculiar to self-righteous idealists, they decided to let the famine run its course with the idea that it would teach the peasants a lesson.''

The fourth step was the process of the dilution of the country's ethnic character through mass resettlement of non-Ukrainians by moving thousands of its population into the empty villages. In this way, ethnic unity was destroyed and nationalities mixed. "Between 1920 and 1939, the population of Ukraine changed from 80% Ukrainian to only 63%. In the face of famine and deportation, the Ukrainian population had declined absolutely from 23.2 million to 19.6 million, while the non-Ukrainian population had increased by 5.6 million. When we consider that Ukraine once had the highest rate of population increase in Europe, around 800,000 per year, it is easy to see that the Russian policy has been accomplished.

This is not simply a case of mass murder. It is a case of genocide, of destruction, not of individuals only, but of a culture and a nation."

In 2006 the Ukrainian Parliament accepted the Law "About the Holodomor of 1932-1933 in Ukraine" in which Holodomor is recognized as Genocide against Ukrainian people.

In 2010, Kiev Court of Appeal in Kiev recognized the genocidal nature of Holodomor, based on the collective intention of Stalin, Molotov, Kaganovich, Postyshev, Chubar, Khatayevych, Kosior to destroy a part of the Ukrainian nation. In 1932 - 1933 the Ukrainians were killed not just in the Ukrainian SSR, but also in the regions which were historically populated by the Ukrainians: the Kuban, the North Caucasus, Lower Volga and Kazakhstan.

Despite Russia's anger, some countries such as Canada, Argentina, Australia and 15 others recognized Holodomor as the deliberate act of Genocide against Ukraine.

On 22 May 2017, the Washington State Senate approved a resolution calling Holodomor "genocide by Stalin's regime against the people of Ukraine", making Washington the first of the US States to call it Genocide.

12.   How Moscow bred Hitler

After the World War I, the Treaty of Versailles limited German Army number to 100 thousand men and forbade Germany from producing or purchasing airplanes, armored vehicles, and submarines. By these restrictions, Entente intended to keep Germany's hopes for military revenge under control. On its side, German Higher Command started looking for the ways to secretly revive its military might or even increase it.

Within a year they found another country also dissatisfied with the WW I outcome and which was open for military cooperation with Germany - the Soviet Union.

During secret talks in Moscow in 1920, Trotsky indicated that they would even consent in recognizing the German borders of 1914 which meant partitioning of Poland.

It means that the roots, the initial scheming of Molotov-Ribbentrop Act of dividing Poland of 1939 lay 20 before.

After WW 1 Bolshevik Russia needed technologies badly including military ones for further "wars of working-class liberation", Germany needed the places to test and even produce the military equipment, and so the secret cooperation was initiated without any delay.

Already in 1926 the West was shocked to discover of the huge Junkers aircraft production plant situated right on the Moscow outskirt.

To test the planes and to teach pilots to fly these machines, a Flying School was created not far from Moscow in the city of Lipetsk. German and Russian pilots lived, flew and studied together there.

Several hundred pilots and aircraft mechanics who went through that school will become the core of German Luftwaffe during WW II.

Farther to the east from Moscow, in the city of Kazan Armored Vehicle School was opened. The future commanders of German tank divisions such as Guderian not only attended it but even taught there. The German tank prototypes were tested at the School as well. Major German corporations such as Krupp, Daimler, and M.A.N. sent their engineering teams to Kazan for the field-testing of future WW II German tanks prototypes.

In two cities - Podosinki near Moscow, and Tomka near Samara - two chemical facilities functioned where two sides worked on creating chemical weapons.

"While Soviet-German military cooperation between 1922 and 1933 is often forgotten, it had a decisive impact on the origins and outbreak of World War II. Germany rebuilt its shattered military at four secret bases hidden in Russia. In exchange, the Reichswehr sent men to teach and train the young Soviet officer corps. However, the most important aspect of Soviet-German cooperation was its technological component. Together, the two states built a network of laboratories, workshops, and testing grounds in which they developed what became the major weapons systems of World War II. Without the technical results of this cooperation, Hitler would have been unable to launch his wars of conquest." - writes Ian Johnson Ph.D., a doctoral fellow with International Security Studies at Yale University in his work "Sowing the Wind: The First Soviet-German Military Pact and the Origins of World War II"

In 1940 year alone, Moscow delivered to Germany 2 thousand aviation bombs with weight from 500 to 1000 kilograms for bombing England.

Goebbels wrote in his diary: "Russians deliver us more than we even wanted. Stalin does everything for us to like him." Quote from the same diary as of April 14, 1941: "Stalin embraces the German

Military Attaché and declares that Russia and Germany will march together to their goal. This is marvelous and for the moment extremely useful. We shall bring it to the notice of English with all appropriate force."

And May 10, 1941: ""Moscow has declared that it no longer recognises Belgium and Norway as sovereign states. Handed their ambassadors their marching-orders. So things have reached that stage. O Nightingale, I hear you twitter. But it will not do Stalin much good now."

Stalin also granted the German Navy permission to use a secret naval base near Murmansk to follow British shipping and make German invasion of Norway easier.

Why did Stalin do all that? It does not seem logical that he wanted to breed another military power on the continent, especially close to his borders, does it? Logical is the thought that Stalin wanted for Hitler to start the war in Europe, exhaust the military resources of all sides, and then capture the whole continent as a "liberator".

"Long before his rising to power, the Soviet leaders gave Hitler a secret title: Icebreaker of the Revolution," – writes in his *Icebreaker* book Victor Suvorov. The book is irrefutable in providing evidence that Red Army was already in position and ready to attack Germany and Romania and Hitler simply got ahead of it.

Note of Interest.   Some German weapons engineers worked in Russia after the WW II. Not many people in the West know that Hugo Schmeisser, one of the best gun specialists in the world worked at Izhevsk plant for many years.

Hugo Schmeisser. Schmeisser is most famous for the world's first MP18 submachine gun, and the world's first assault rifle MP43/44 "Sturmgewehr."

During WW II he created Stg-44 semi-automatic gun. In 1945 the USSR confiscated thousands of sheets of its design and even made 50 StG44s from the available parts.

The USSR also forced Hugo Schmeisser to work at an Izhevsk plant near Kazan for 7 years until 1952.

And, - what a coincidence! - at the very time an unknown Russian genius with no engineering achievements whatsoever named Mikhail Kalashnikov invents an automatic gun that looks exactly like the Hugo's Stg-44!

The two guns look so alike to non-specialist, that there happened a great scandal when on the monument to Kalashnikov opened in Moscow in 2017, the designers installed a Stg-44 scheme instead of AKM-47.

Here is another question of the kind - what could German physicist Manfred Von Ardenne receive two Stalin Prizes and the Order of Lenin for? Right after the successful test of the Soviet atomic A-bomb? There were also physical chemists Max Volmer, Max Steenbeck, and Nobel laureate in Physics Gustav Hertz who worked beside him on the project near Moscow and in the city of Sukhumy on the Black Sea. It is to Sukhumy, Ardenne moved his cyclotron and uranium centrifuge on which he tried to create an atomic bomb for the Fuhrer during WWII.

The former I. G. Farben complex southeast of Berlin already in 1947 "was shipping the phenomenal quantity of 30 tons of distilled metallic calcium per month—at the time, total US production of calcium was 3–5 tons per year, - onward to Zaporizhe (Ukraine) on the Dnieper River," – CIA reported. "There could be no non-nuclear use for so much calcium in such a pure form."

Apart from appropriating Ukrainian inventions, Russia appropriated some German ones too.

13.   Ukraine - Hitler's main purpose of WW II, "Volga - Mississippi"

"The purpose of the Second World War, from Hitler's point of view, was the conquest of Ukraine. It is therefore senseless to commemorate any part of the Second World War without beginning from Ukraine. Any commemoration of the Second World War which involves the Nazi purposes — the ideological, economic, and political purposes of the Nazi regime — must begin precisely from Ukraine.

This is not only a matter of theory, this is a matter of practice. German policies, the policies that we remember, all of them focus precisely on Ukraine: The Hunger Plan, with its notion that tens of millions of people were going to starve in the winter of 1941; Generalplan Ost, with its idea that millions more people would be forcibly transported or killed in the 5, 10, or 15 years to follow, but also the Final Solution, Hitler's idea of the elimination of Jews; all of these policies hung together in theory and in practice, with the idea of an invasion of the Soviet Union, the major goal of which would be the conquest of Ukraine."

This is an exact transcript, quotation of a Yale History Professor Timothy Snyder's speech in German Bundestag on 20 June 2017.

According to Dr. Snyder, right before his attack on the Soviet Union Hitler knew that 90% (!) percent of the food shipments from the Soviet Union came from Soviet Ukraine. Even after the purges and Holodomor, Ukraine continued to feed Soviet Russia and the rest of the Soviet Union.

In August 1940 the German army general staff had analytics at hand proving that Ukraine was "agriculturally and industrially the most valuable part of the Soviet Union."

Hitler also wanted to occupy Ukraine "so that no one is able to starve us again, like in the last war." The conquest of Ukraine would, according to German plans, first insulate Germany from the British blockade, and then the colonization of Ukraine would allow Germany to become a global power on the model of the United States.

It was the model of the early United States, or namely the model of frontier colonialism, a frontier empire built by slave labor, that was admired by Adolf Hitler.

So the questions Hitler asked were: who will the racial inferiors be? Who will the slaves be in the German Eastern Empire?

"And the answer that he gave, both in Mein Kampf, and in his second book, and in practice with the invasion of 1941, the answer was: the Ukrainians.

The Ukrainians were to be at the center of a project of colonization and enslavement. The Ukrainians were to be treated as Afrikaner, or as Neger — the word was very often used, as those of you who read German documents from the war will know — by analogy with the United States. The idea was to create a slavery-driven, exterminatory, colonial regime in Eastern Europe where the center was going to be Ukraine."

And the Volga River in Russia, as Hitler once proclaimed, would become Germany's Mississippi.

Food from Ukraine was to be sent not to Russia or the rest of the Soviet Union but solely to Germany and then resold to the rest of Europe.

Ukraine, in German view, was a "surplus region" meaning it produced more food than it needed. Russia and Belarus were "deficit regions." After the German occupation, inhabitants of Ukrainian cities, and almost everyone in Belarus and in northwestern Russia would have to starve to death or flee.

In the winter of 1941-1942 alone, according to German calculations, 30 million were to starve to death. As a result of population extinction, the cities would have been destroyed and the terrain would be returned to natural forest.

This Hunger Plan shows why Hitler never planned to conquer any more than 10% of Soviet Russia, and in reality, German armies never captured more than 5% of Soviet Russia.

As a result, Ukraine, greatly weakened by Stalin's Holodomor, would become the major battlefield of the WW II.

As shown above, lives of tens of millions Russians and Belorussians depended on the outcome of what was happening in Ukraine.

The future of Europe and, probably, the whole world too.

Point of interest

Führerhauptquartier Werwolf is the codename used for one of Adolf Hitler's World War II Eastern Front military headquarters located in a pine forest about 12 kilometers (7.5 miles) north of Vinnytsia, Ukraine, which was used between 1942 and 1943. It was one of a number of Führer Headquarters throughout Europe, but the most easterly ever used by Hitler in person.

Actually, out of three stays, the first one in 1942 was the longest – from the middle of July to the end of October. Three and half months. The Stalingrad Plan was elaborated and issued in this place during that time.

14.   Ukraine - the Major Battlefield of WW II

"More Ukrainians fought and died on the Allied side than French, British and Americans put together. Why do we not see this? Because we forget that Ukrainians were fighting in the Red Army. We confuse the Red Army with the Russian Army, which it most definitely was not.

The Red Army was the army of the Soviet Union, in which Ukrainians, because of the geography of the war were substantially over-represented," - it is the same Yale History Professor Timothy Snyder during his speech at German Bundestag.

In relative terms, Ukrainians constituted around 40% of Red Army soldiers and 3 million of them died during WW II.

In addition to those casualties, 3.5 million mostly women and children became victims of German killing policies between 1941 and 1945.

Such heavy losses on part of Ukraine Dr. Snyder explains by two conditions.

The first was that Ukraine was the major war aim, the center of Hitler's ideological ambitions.

Second, Ukraine was occupied for most of the war.

So, in absolute numbers, more inhabitants of Ukraine died in the WW II than the inhabitants of Soviet Russia even according to Russian historians. Which means that in relative terms, Ukraine lost and suffered far, far more during the war than Soviet Russia.

Another shocking truth is that even during WW II Russians continued killing Ukrainian civilians for nothing.

In 1941, as Nazi German troops were approaching the Dnieper River, Josef Stalin's secret police blew up a hydroelectric dam in the city of Zaporizhia. The explosion sent a huge tsunami-size wave down the current sweeping villages along the banks. No less than 100 thousand Ukrainians perished in the hand-made tsunami.

Current Russia makes every effort to present itself to the world as liberators, and Ukrainians - as collaborators.

There truly were some Ukrainians who took the arms and went to revenge Russians for Holodomor and other purges, but their number was correspondent with the proportions of other smaller nations. For the whole Ukraine there were roughly 50 thousand who fought on side of the Nazi.

A much greater number in Western Ukraine fought against both Hitler and Stalin and continued a guerrilla war with the Soviets up until 1953, - 8 years after the war ended!

It's about these fighters Charles de Gaulle once said, "If I had an army like the Ukrainian Insurgent Army, the German boot would have never trodden on French soil."

Who collaborated the most of all the former USSR nations?

The Russian Liberation Army, or Vlasov Army alone fighting on the side of Hitler counted 300 thousand at its peak. There were other formations and the total number of Russian collaborators with Nazi was above 1 million.

In 2010 Putin declared that Russia would have won the WW II even without Ukraine.

Looking at how the whole USSR barely survived "by the skin of the teeth" at the brink of Volga in Stalingrad, it is clear that without Ukrainian contribution Russia would have found itself behind the Urals mountains. Where it would have starved to death as Hitler had planned.

With all the facts at hand now and understanding the reason Putin wanted to appropriate the Victory in WW II before his assault on Ukraine in 2014, there is a short answer to that claim:

Without Russia's decades-long collaboration with Germans before WW II, without the Molotov-Ribbentrop Pact, there would not have been any WW II in the first place!

Millions of Ukrainians, hundreds thousands of Americans, British and other nationalities would have stayed alive.

Vital to Remember!

Couple of words on the consequences of the Molotov-Ribbentrop Pact for Poland in the years 1939-1941.

"The Soviets claimed that their intervention was necessary because the Polish state had ceased to exist. Since Poland could no longer protect its own citizens, went the argument, the Red Army had to enter the country on a peacekeeping mission. Poland's large Ukrainian and Belarusian minorities, went the Soviet propaganda, were in particular need of rescue," writes Dr. Snyder in his book "Bloodlands."

Does the Soviets rhetoric resemble the words of Putin before invading Crimea and Donbas in 2014? Only this time it was "the Russians" to be protected.

"In the background, the NKVD entered the country, in force. In the twenty-one months to come it made more arrests in occupied eastern Poland than in the entire Soviet Union, seizing some 109,400 Polish citizens. The typical sentence was eight years in the Gulag; about 8,513 people were sentenced to death."

That is how the typical "Russian peacekeeping mission" looks.

It was to one of such places where Polish officers were massacred by NKVD, the Poland's President with his wife and some other 90 top officials were flying on April 10, 2010. The place they were heading to is called Katyn, where more than 22 thousand Polish officers were shot in 1940.

The plane with the Polish delegation crashed leaving no one alive. For some time the dense fog that morning was thought to be the reason of the crash, although the way Russia treated the debris of the crash was raising suspicions already then.

In April 2018, Poland's ex-Minister of National Defense Antoni Macierewicz, who now heads the Polish sub-commission investigating the crash of a Tu-154 plane with former Polish President Lech Kaczynski and other senior officials of Poland in Russia's Smolensk in 2010, declared that the official cause behind the death of the crash victims was an explosion that occurred before the plane hit the ground.

Was Poland the only country the USSR invaded or tried to invade in that period? There was also the Winter War with Finland in 1939 which started with the false flag Mainila accident in which NKVD shelled the Russian village to receive the casus belli. By different estimates, during the 105-days war, Finland lost close to 26 000 dead or missing, while Soviet losses equaled 168 000 killed or missing. The territories Moscow annexed as a result of the war, are still occupied by Russia.

There was also the occupation of the Baltic States – Estonia, Latvia, Lithuania, and occupation of Bessarabia and Northern Bukovina.

15.   The Largest Tank Battle in History. Not Kursk

"This Was the Biggest and Baddest Tank Battle of All Time," named his article for The National Interest 2019 issue Robert Beckhusen. He also provided the numbers: "The battle which developed and then concluded on June 30 was a confusing morass that swallowed 2,648 Soviet tanks out of a total force of 5,000 versus some 1,000 German tanks."

It was June 30 of 1941, next week after Nazi Germany invaded the Soviet Union on June 22, 1941. That week between Dubno, Lutsk and Brody in western Ukraine, six Soviet mechanized corps launched a counter attack into the advancing 1st Panzer Group advancing toward Kiev.

Why was so little information about this battle? Was it concealed on purpose? Looks like it truly was.

The Soviets may have hidden the truth about the Brody battle because otherwise, they would have to give answers to some inconvenient questions.

For example, where did so many tanks come from if the USSR was not preparing for the war as they like to tell everybody?

What were so many tanks doing almost on the border with the countries like Hungary and Romania? Tanks are surely not a defensive type of weaponry.

Maybe those were some old tanks?

"What's all the more remarkable is that the Soviet corps had considerable numbers of heavier KV and T-34 tanks, tougher than the German army's best tanks at the time. The Soviet 10th Tank Division of the 15th Mechanized Corps alone had 63 KVs and 38 T-34s," quotes Robert Beckhusen an American military historian David Glantz. The availability of such tanks already in 1941 shows how "not ready for the war" the Soviet Union in reality was.

Now a quick look at the Kursk tank battle, also known as the Battle at Prokhorovka, which took place two years later, in 1943. How many tanks did it involve? There were not the popular common figures of 1,500 tanks Russia claimed. Not even 1,000.

In 2019, a British historian Ben Wheatley analyzed Luftwaffe aerial photos of the Prokhorovka battlefield, taken on 14-16 July. The photos were found in the US National Archives at College Park, Maryland.

His verdict was that the battle so steeped in Soviet legend for many decades was, in fact, a Soviet armored disaster.

.Wheatley's report starts with providing different numbers of the tanks: "On the morning of 12 July,... 672 Soviet fighting vehicles were effectively engaged that day in action against the 200 tanks, assault guns and tank destroyers of divisions Leibstandarte and Das Reich."

And this is how the battle ended "The battlefield remained largely unaltered from 12 July. As a result, these photographs depict the Soviet armored disaster (the entire 5th Guards Tank Army **lost around 235 fighting vehicles** written off) with absolute clarity.

...German tank losses were minuscule by comparison, with just **five battle tanks** ultimately being written off."

Wheatley and a German military historian, Karl-Heinz Frieser, were cited in a feature in the German daily Die Welt, and, as BBC reports, "it hit a Russian raw nerve".

German journalist of Die Welt, Sven Felix Kelleroff, found the evidence of Soviet humiliation so convincing, that he called on Russians to demolish the Victory Monument, erected in memory of the tank battle on Prokhorovka field. He expressed this opinion in his article published in the newspaper Die Welt.

"In fact, this monument should have been demolished immediately. Because the latest research, based on undoubtedly real photographs, confirms: Prokhorovka had neither a Soviet victory nor even a grand tank battle," he wrote.

KV-1 (abbrev. Kliment Voroshilov) 45-ton heavy tank

16.   How US First Lady befriended Lady Death

Confirmed 309 kills, including 100 German officers and 36 German snipers.

Lyudmila Pavlichenko was born in 1916 in Bila Tserkva, a Ukranian town just outside of Kiev.

She was 24-year-old history student at Kiev University when the war started.

In just a little more than a year, on a U.S. tour in 1942 already highly decorated and renown lieutenant, she will find a friend in the First Lady.

She was sent to the US on a mission to call on Americans to open a "second front" in Europe. Stalin desperately needed for the United States to send its troops to Europe and distract German forces, so that the Red Army could get some relief.

Lyudmila Pavlichenko visited with President Franklin Roosevelt and became the first Soviet citizen to be received at the White House by a U.S. President.

After the reception, Eleanor Roosevelt asked the young officer to accompany her on a tour of the country and tell Americans of her experiences as a woman and a soldier.

Although the New York Times dubbed her the "Girl Sniper," by that time Pavlichenko had been wounded four times and had already become the most feared female sniper in history.

She readily accepted the first lady's offer.

In just a little while, Pavlichenko was already telling the American audiences in different States the stories how she became a sniper and of the devastating effect of the war on her homeland.

Her sniping hobby actually started before the war, - right after she had enrolled at Kiev University with an intent to become a school teacher.

There, she competed as a sprinter, pole vaulter, and, "to perfect myself at shooting, I took courses at a sniper's school," she said.

When the war broke out, the skill came handy - during an impromptu audition held not at a shooting range, but in the vicinity of the enemy, she was handed a rifle and was pointed at a pair of Romanians at a distance who were working with the Germans.

"When I picked off the two, I was accepted," Pavlichenko recalled.

She was immediately enlisted and given her weapon - a Mosin-Nagant 7.62 mm rifle with a PE 4x telescope.

She managed to have 187 confirmed kills in her first 75 days of the war during the fierce fighting at Odessa, Ukraine.

Eventually, as her kill count was rising, she was given more and more dangerous assignments, including the riskiest of all—counter-sniping.

Pavlichenko won all 36 sniper duels which at times could last all day and all night. One duel lasted for three days.

That last one supposedly was the duel against one of the more decorated snipers in history. It is said that the log with over 500 confirmed kills was found on him after the duel was over in Pavlichenko's favor.

15 years after that trip across America, Eleanor Roosevelt came to Moscow. It was already the Cold War period, so Roosevelt's agenda was quite restricted. Still, the former First Lady persisted in paying a

visit to her old friend Lyudmila Pavlichenko who at the time lived in Moscow.

At the meeting, when they managed to get alone, two women embraced, and half-laughing, half-crying told each other how happy they were to see each other again.

It must have been some special friendship between the US First Lady and the Ukrainian girl who had to become a war veteran at such a young age to prove so enduring.

Wondering about all this, - about what could have brought about a friendship so strong between the women of so different cultures and so different status, wondering what could have made the journalists change so drastically their attitude toward Pavlichenko from the initial distrust disguised in semi-mocking questions about Lyudmila's uniform, hair, lips and style and replace it by applauds and admiration closer to the end of her US tour, only one thing comes to mind - the similarity.

The inner one.

As mentioned in previous chapters, Ukraine as such was formed as a borderland, as constant battlefield guarding European civilization against nomads in the first place.

The United States also had its borderlands - Bad Lands (I've been there - quite a scary place even nowadays), Wild West, etc.

Just like in Ukraine, in the United States, not just men had to become the best at using weapons to survive and defend their families. Women had to master arms as well.

Also, another thing that must have gained American audience was the fact that the best lady sniper in the world history turned out to be basically an amateur. Somehow it is hard to imagine the audience feeling or supporting a specially trained killing machine.

But Pavlichenko was a typical Ukrainian lady with the dreams to become a history teacher, but with hobbies that required precision. Forced by war, she simply had to utilize one of them. But for the war, she would have excelled at something else. All this relates in many senses to the American Dream - one can reach and accomplish the impossible if one does it with one's heart and mind. In such a case, an amateur will beat professionals, a lady will outperform men, a prey will become a merciless hunter.

And that is what, in my opinion, "struck the chord" between the different nations, between Ukrainian and American women in the first place.

Including the First Lady, Mrs. Eleanor Roosevelt.

In 1942 American folk singer Woody Guthrie wrote a song, "Miss Pavlichenko."

In 2015 a jointly produced film by Ukraine and Russia describing the events in greater detail was released. It was a year of the aggression of Russia against Ukraine, so the countries had different names for the movie.

Ukraine named it "The Invincible" because there were truly certain moments in Pavlichenko's military career where it is simply a miracle how she survived.

Russia decided to call the movie "Battle for Sevastopol."

Why such a name? A most obvious answer is that they seemed eager to distract the attention of the viewers from the main character of the film -the Ukrainian distinguished sniper.

Also, they wanted to remind of the sacrifices "the Russians" paid defending Crimea.

But in Sevastopol, other nations and nationalities may have been the majority. There is no proof that those were the Russian soldiers who carried the heaviest burden in that battle or paid the crucial role in defending the city.

What was there Russian for sure – it is the attitude toward the soldiers when the high command escaped like rats from the sinking ship, and Sevastopol became the perfect example of anti-Dunkirk.

17.   Frau Black Death, Encounter at the Elbe

Another outstanding Ukrainian lady-warrior was Yevdokia Zavaliy. Actually, she is the one who could be called a "Girl". Being only 16 at the beginning of the War, in just three years she will become the ONLY WOMAN in the whole Red Army during WW2 to command a marine squad.

The Germans will call her "Lady Black Death."

Born in 1924 in a small village in the Mykolaiv region of Ukraine, Yevdokia worked on a farm from her childhood years.

The outbreak of World War II when enemy planes bombed her village was brutal to her. After the bombing, she had to treat injured soldiers making improvised bandages of her bed sheets, and it had such a strong impression on her that she persuaded a regiment commander to take her with them to the front line, claiming to be 18 years old when she, in fact, was only 16.

At first, Zavaliy served as a nurse but quickly learned to shoot rifles, pistols and machine guns. Very soon she herself was wounded to the abdomen while dragging a wounded officer to safety. She was awarded the Order of the Red Star for her bravery for this feat.

One day Zavaliy was mistaken for a male soldier since she was bold at the time and wore a typical uniform. She was ordered to join a group of soldiers going to the front line. Yevdokia decided not to reveal who she was and went on with her new identity.

In one of the many battles that followed, she captured a German officer in combat and was appointed to the command of a reconnaissance squad.

In yet another incident, she schemed a dangerous night raid across the river to a German camp to steal provision to feed her starving companions.

In yet another battle her company was surrounded and her commander was killed during the heavy firefight. Zavaliy took command and in some daring maneuver broke the enemy encirclement saving her companions but getting severely injured again. Of course, during surgery, the doctors discovered that she was a female.

Still, despite many prejudices, because of her prior achievements, she was even promoted to commander of a gunner platoon.

The men of the platoon were reluctant in the beginning to follow the orders from a girl, but Zavaliy quickly earned their respect.

She also made Germans fear her to the extent they called her Frau Black Death - "black" most likely for the black color of her artillery uniform.

Through all her military career Yevdokia Zavaliy received close to 40 medals of Honor.

After the war she settled in Kiev where she married, had 2 children and lived a peaceful life working as a grocery store manager. She passed away only several years ago - in 2010.

Note of interest. There is also the best scoring pilot of the Allied Forces a Ukrainian Ivan Kozhedub who needs to be at least briefly mentioned here.

Also, when I asked a Reddit community "Ask an American" a question what Americans of Ukrainian origin the readers happen to know, one of the answers was this:

"For conspicuous gallantry and intrepidity at risk of life above and beyond the call of duty, on 23 May 1944, near Ponte Rotto, Italy. Pfc. John W. Dutko left the cover of an abandoned enemy trench at the height of an artillery concentration in a single-handed attack upon 3 machineguns and an 88mm. mobile gun. Despite the intense fire of these 4 weapons which were aimed directly at him, Pfc. Dutko ran 10.0 yards through the impact area, paused momentarily in a shell crater, and then continued his 1-man assault. Although machinegun bullets kicked up the dirt at his heels, and 88mm. shells exploded within 30 yards of him, Pfc. Dutko nevertheless made his way to a point within 30 yards of the first enemy machinegun and killed both gunners with a hand grenade. Although the second machinegun wounded him, knocking him to the ground, Pfc. Dutko regained his feet and advanced on the 88mm. gun, firing his Browning automatic rifle from the hip. When he came within 10 yards of this weapon he killed its 5-man crew with 1 long burst of fire. Wheeling on the machinegun which had wounded him, Pfc. Dutko killed the gunner and his assistant. The third German machinegun fired on Pfc. Dutko from a position 20 yards distant wounding him a second time as he proceeded toward the enemy weapon in a half run. He killed both members of its crew with a single burst from his Browning automatic rifle, continued toward the gun and died, his body falling across the dead German crew."

Here is another Ukrainian-American described by Wikipedia:

"On January 23, 1945, near Tettingen, Germany, Master Sergeant Nicholas Oresko single-handedly and under enemy fire, took out a German bunker position that was armed with a machine gun. Seriously wounded by another enemy machine gun from another bunker, he attacked that bunker under fire and destroyed that enemy position. Nine months later on October 30, 1945, he was awarded the Medal of Honor. President Harry Truman formally presented Oresko the medal during a ceremony at the White House."

The Encounter at the Elbe happened between the American troops and the First Ukrainian front by the way and it is Ukrainian Alexander Silvashko you can see on one of the iconic photographs of the WWII. Silvashko joined the infantry and went to the front from the Cherkassy Region of Ukraine, where he was born. He was wounded three times and once suffered concussion. Ater Torgau there were Dresden and Prague. When he was back to his homeland, it was starving dreadfully, so he travelled to Belarus to exchange some of his possessions for food and stayed there. He worked as a school teacher.

18. Turbojet and Turbofan Engines

In 1926, a young man from Kiev region entered Kiev Polytechnic Institute, the same Institute, in which Igor Sikorsky and Konstantin Kalinin studied before him. The man's first name was Arkhip, his last name was Lyulka, which in Ukrainian means *cradle*.

After graduation, Arkhip moved to Kharkov and started teaching at Aeronautical Institute. It was the time and the same city where Konstantin Kalinin was test flying his K-7. In 1938, in Kharkov Lyulka theoretically designed a gas-turbine engine, - GTD. A bit later, he designed the first turbojet engine of the USSR.

Quick explanation. Turbojet is a simple turbine engine in which all of the air passes through the turbine. It is quite inefficient since it burns a lot of fuel. All of its thrust comes from the exhaust from the turbine section. British engineer Frank Whittle patented the jet engine idea in 1930 after the Air Ministry turned him down.

In April 1941, Arkhip Lyulka patented what was to become the first double-jet turbofan engine in the world.

Turbofan is different from turbojet in that it has a fan at the front of the engine. Part of the air enters the turbine section of the engine, and the rest bypasses around the engine. This bypass air creates additional thrust, cools the engine, and makes the engine quieter. The bypass air produces the majority of an engine's thrust.

Although several prototypes were built and ready for the tests already in 1941, Arkhip Lyulka was forced to abandon the project and evacuate to the Urals because of the German invasion.

Soviet space aircraft designer Academician Boris Chertok in his memoirs *Rockets and People* recalls the first time he met Arkhip Lyulka during that period: "Lyulka personally explained to me the differences between the two classes of reactive engines – liquid-propellant rocket engines and turbojet engines. He did not disparage liquid-propellant rocket engines, which had to carry their own fuel and oxidizer. But with gentle humor, alternating Russian speech with melodious Ukrainian, of which he had a beautiful command, Arkhip Lyulka proved that everything had its place while telling me about the turbojet engine."

In 1945, Lyulka designed the first Soviet jet engine, TR-1 which was established on Su-11 fighter jets.

In 1946, the OKB-165 experimental design bureau was established in Moscow to develop Soviet turbojet engines, and Arkhip Lyulka was appointed the manager of it. The engines designed by the bureau came to be named with the initial letters AL designating Arkhip Lyulka.

Lyulka design bureau created many successful turbojet engines, which powered the Sukhoi, Tupolev and Ilyushin aircraft.

One of the engines, AL-21F, needs to be mentioned briefly separately. This engine was so similar in power and technology to the General Electric J79, the first engine for supersonic flight, that the Western aviation specialists believed AL-21 was designed by reverse engineering a J-79 from an F-4 Phantom plane shot down in Vietnam. But after the fall of the USSR, it became clear that AL-21F3 was different and even exceeded J-79.

In the early 1970s, Arkhip Lyulka returned to his invention - the double-jet turbofan engine design, the certificate of authorship for which he received in 1941.

In 1976, the A. Lyulka design bureau created the AL-31F 4th generation engine. This engine would become the peak of Lyulka's work. This engine was installed on the Su-27 aircraft, on which from 1986 to 1988 more than 30 world records were established.

It is considered one of the best engines in the world for the front-line aviation. The AL-31F was fitted to the Su-33 carrier-borne fighters, the Su-35 multi-purpose fighters, the Su-30MK, and the Su-34 front-line bombers. The engine powers also the Chengdu J-10 multirole jet fighter developed by China.

Nowadays, the absolute majority of gas-turbine engines in the world are built based on the Ukrainian innovator's design.

Point of Interest

Academician Boris Chertok in his book mentions the beginning of cooperation between Arkhip Lyulka and the father of the USSR space program: "Korolev was already acquainted with Lyulka from the Academy of Sciences. He had several meetings with him, persuading him to work on the development of a liquid-hydrogen rocket engine. I heard that Korolev was quite enthralled with Lyulka's distinctive Russian-Ukrainian diction."

Why Sergei Korolev was enthralled with Lyulka's Ukrainian diction is in the next chapter.

19.   Space Race vs. Battered Ukrainian Genius

At approximately the time Lyudmila Pavlichenko was on a US tour, another Ukrainian was in Moscow prison having only recently been transferred from GULAG.

It was a strange prison in many ways, first of all, because of the large number of drawings of the planes, engines, and rockets everywhere.

The prisoner was one of many who worked on the drawings and his name was Sergei Korolev. The man who in less than 20 years will open space to Humankind and send Gagarin into cosmos.

The man who would open space to humankind, Sergei Pavlovich Korolev, was born on 12 January 1907 (30 Dec 1906 old calendar), in Zhitomir, Ukraine.

His mother Maria Mykolayivna Moskalenko, was a Ukrainian from Nizhyn. His father Pavel Korolev had originally come to Zhytomyr from Mogilev, Belarus to be a teacher of Russian language.

Three years after his birth the couple separated, and Sergei never saw his father again - he was told by his mother that his father had died, and only later learned that Pavel lived until 1929 and even wrote to Maria requesting a meeting with his son.

Korolev grew up in Nizhyn, under the care of his maternal grandparents Mykola Moskalenko and Maria Moskalenko (Fursa), a daughter of a local Cossack.

In short, Sergei grew up in a fully Ukrainian environment with the influence of the Ukrainian Cossacks traditions. It is important to know.

In 1915 his mother got a divorce and in 1916 married Grigory Balanin, an electrical engineer with German education, attending Kiev Polytechnic University.

Grigory proved a good influence on Sergei. In 1917 the family had to move to Odessa where Grigory received the job with the regional railway.

That is where Sergei's interest in aeronautical engineering started getting momentum. In 1923 he joined the Society of Aviation and Aerial Navigation of Ukraine and the Crimea (OAVUK). He had his first flying lesson and flew as a passenger numerous times during that period of time also.

KIEV

To develop his interest, in 1924 he enters Kiev Polytechnic Institute because it had an aviation branch.

It is the Institute where Konstantin Kalinin, the future designer studies at the time. And it is where Igor Sikorsky studied some 10 years earlier.

In Kiev, Sergei lived with his uncle on mother's side Yuri and earned money to pay for his courses by doing various jobs. At the courses, he met and became attracted to a classmate, Xenia Vincentini, who would later become his first wife.

While entering Kiev institute, Sergei Korolev filled in the Application Form. It is filled in perfect Ukrainian language and in the Application Sergei Korolev states his nationality as Ukrainian.

RUSSIA

Having completed his 2nd year in Kiev, in July 1926, Sergei Korolev was accepted into the Bauman Moscow State Technical University. His diploma advisor there was Andrei Tupolev.

By 1930 Korolev became a lead engineer on the Tupolev TB-3 heavy bomber.

In 1931, together with Friedrich Zander, a space travel enthusiast, he participated in the creation of the Group for the Study of Reactive Motion (GIRD). In 1933, the group accomplished their first launch of a liquid-fueled rocket, which was called GIRD-X.

At that stage, the military became interested in the work of the group and began providing some funding.

In 1933, it was decided by the government to merge GIRD with the Gas Dynamics Laboratory (GDL) in Leningrad. Thus, the Jet Propulsion Research Institute (RNII) was created with Korolev becoming the Deputy Chief of the institute. He led the development of cruise missiles and a manned rocket-powered glider. Another great Ukrainian spacecraft engineer - Valentin Glushko was on his team as well.

GULAG

On 27 June 1938, during the Great Purge, NKVD agents broke into Korolev's apartment and arrested him as a spy.

Having been severely beaten and with his jaw broken, Korolev was forced to admit to crimes of treason and sabotage which he had not committed. The jaw most likely was broken in that instance when Sergei Korolev asked for a glass of water and the interrogator smashed the jug in his face.

That day, according to NKVD officer's Interrogation Report, Sergei Korolev suddenly becomes "Russian".

Korolev was sentenced to 10 years' of hard labor at the Kolyma gold mine, the most notorious of all Gulag prison camps.

One year later though, at the end of 1939, he was sent back to Moscow. During that one year, he had already sustained injuries and had lost most of his teeth because of the camp's brutal conditions.

When he reached Moscow, his sentence was reduced to eight years, which he did not have to serve in a labor camp. Instead, there was another sort of prison.

Korolev was still very fortunate to have even survived because his other RNII colleagues had been already executed by the time. That is how the Soviet rocket program was set back and fell behind the German one.

"Another egregious example of the incredible stupidity, not to speak of callous cruelty, of the purges of Joseph Stalin", writes Korolev's biographer James Harford in his book.

СП. Королев в Бутырской тюрьме на следующий день после возвращения с Колымы. 29 февраля 1940 г.

"Korolev in a Moscow prison the next day after his return from Kolyma (GULAG), Feb. 29, 1940"

"SHARASHKA"

Korolev was assigned to a "sharashka", a penitentiary where scientists and engineers worked on different military projects.

For example, the first "sharashka" where Korolev worked, served as Tupolev's engineering facility which designed both the Tupolev Tu-2 bomber and the Petlyakov Pe-2 dive bomber.

His second "sharashka" where he managed to transfer to in 1942, worked under aforementioned Valentin Glushko and designed rocket-assisted takeoff boosters for aircraft.

Korolev was kept in the "sharashka" and isolated from his family until 1944, the time, when he, along with Tupolev, Glushko, and others was finally discharged by special government decree. The charges against him were not dropped until 1957 though.

BALLISTIC MISSILE

In 1954 Korolev's design bureau produced the first ballistic missile with a nuclear charge, - the R-5. Two years later it constructed the first intercontinental two-stage ballistic missile, - the R-7. This missile became the basis for all of today's rocket carriers.

SPUTNIK (and not received Nobel Prize)

It is in cooperation with Valentin Glushko, Sergei Korolev managed to launch the first Sputnik October 4, 1957.

The effect of the event was so huge, that the Nobel Committee was ready to award unplanned prizes in 1957. The Kremlin was asked who the sputnik's creators were. Both Korolev and Glushko would have been Nobel Prize winners.

Two Ukrainians – two Nobel Prize holders it would and should have been!

But Nikita Khrushchev pompously answered that the whole Soviet nation was the creator.

Not many people know that the actual design of the Sputnik was very simple and took only one month to build. It consisted of a polished metal sphere, a transmitter, some thermal measuring instruments, batteries and Sergei Korolev basically assembled it alone with his hands barely meeting the deadline.

(It is this shining object assembled by a great Ukrainian would inspire a young coalminer's son in the United States to become a rocket engineer in the famous American movie "October Sky").

SHOOTING THE MOON

It was Korolev's Luna-2 to become the first spacecraft to reach the surface of the Moon, and the first man-made object to land on another celestial body.

On September 13, 1959, it hit the Moon's surface east of Mare Imbrium near the craters Aristides, Archimedes, and Autolycus.

GAGARIN FLIGHT

12 April 1961 is the Date in the history of humankind with the first human in Earth orbit. While there were others to replace Gagarin (German Titov for example), at that time there was no one to replace Korolev. He was in full charge of the process.

SUDDEN DEATH

On 5 January 1966, Korolev was admitted to a hospital for what was supposed to be a routine surgery. But during the operation, on 14 January, he suddenly started to bleed. Doctors tried to provide intubation to allow him to breathe freely, but as they discovered, his jaw broken during the interrogation did not heal properly and impeded the installation of the breathing tube. He never regained consciousness and died, aged 59, later that day.

PLANNED MANNED FLIGHT TO THE MOON

Before his death, Korolev had designed a mighty launcher to carry men to the Moon. The N1, a super-heavy-lift launch vehicle intended to deliver payloads beyond low Earth orbit. Its first stage has been the most powerful rocket stage ever built.

There was also N1-L3 developed to compete with the United States Apollo-Saturn V to land a man on the Moon. It was to use the same Lunar Orbit Rendezvous (LOR) method discussed in the following chapter.

His team continued to work on it but without the Korolev's guidance and inspiration, they failed.

In 1969, just as America was making final preparations for its Apollo missions, two N1 unmanned test launches were carried out.

The first exploded in flight.

The second rocket fell over, destroying the entire launch complex.

Weeks later, the Americans were already on the moon.

Without the Great Ukrainian, the Soviet space leadership halted.

Point of interest

The first song in the history of humankind sung in space and heard on Earth, was a Ukrainian song. It was performed in August 1962, by the first Ukrainian cosmonaut Pavel Popovich on his own initiative for Sergei Korolev and heard by everyone in the Mission Control Center. Popovich knew that it was Korolev's favorite. The song actually made the young Sergei dream of the skies and thus affected his whole life. And not just his, as the history shows.

In Ukrainian it is titled "Dyvlius' Ya Na Nebo" and here is the translation of it:

I'm looking at high skies and it makes me wonder

Why aren't I a falcon? Why aren't I a-flying?

God, why have you left me with no wings to fly?

I'd take off the ground and fly high above

I'd fly over clouds far off a maddening crowd

To look for my fortune, heartache and grief bound

To ask for caress from the moon and the sun

And show off myself in their bright light

And my way to find

Sergei Korolev's daughter, Natalia, recalled: "The very name Ukraine was pronounced in our family with reverence and great love... He (my father) loved Ukraine very much. He loved Ukrainian songs, and he loved Ukrainian language. That is for sure. "I'm looking at high skies" and "The Mighty Dnieper (Roars and Bellows)" were the favorite songs of my grandmother and my father."

20.   Neil Armstrong & handful of soil from Siberia

It may sound unreal, but in the Americans' trip to the Moon and back was a great contribution of Ukrainian intellect too. In fact, it might have been a decisive one:

"In May 1969, with only seven months to go before the end of the decade, the first Lunar Module to fly in orbit around the Moon was powered up and readied for undocking from the Command Module.

Astronauts Tom Stafford, John Young and Gene Cernan were about to test out a technique for lunar landing which had first been proposed in 1916 by a Russian mechanic called Yuri Kondratyuk.

Kondratyuk's thesis described how a small landing craft could leave a mothership in lunar orbit to ferry its crew to the surface and back - a technique later referred to as Lunar Orbit Rendezvous or LOR," reads the BBC article devoted to the 40th Anniversary of the Moon Flight.

BBC was correct as for the influence amateur engineer had on the US mission. They were correct in quoting the year Yuri Kondratyuk made his calculations. But they were wrong about the nationality of the genius - he was Ukrainian.

Yuri Kondratyuk, whose real name was Alexander Sharhey was born in Poltava, Ukraine in 1897.

His father was a Ukrainian, and his mother was a descendant of the Swedish general Schlippenbach who was taken prisoner during the Battle of Poltava mentioned in the first chapter of this book.

The family originally lived in Kiev where Alexander's father, Ignat Benediktovich Sharhey, studied physics and mathematics at Kyiv University which is currently named after Taras Shevchenko.

From his early age, Alexander was fascinated by his father's books on physics and mathematics and demonstrated great abilities in these areas while at school.

Kondratyuk's mother, Ludmila Lvovna Schlippenbach taught French at a Kiev school.

In 1910, when his father died, Aleksandr returned to Poltava to live with his paternal grandmother.

At the outbreak of World War I, he was drafted into the army as a junior officer. It is in those conditions during his time of military service, he filled four notebooks with his ideas of interplanetary flights.

He made detailed calculations of the trajectory to take a spacecraft from Earth orbit to lunar orbit and back to Earth orbit, a trajectory now known as "Kondratyuk's route" or "Kondratyuk's loop".

How and why did Alexander Sharhey become Yuri Kondratyuk?

When the October Revolution started in Russia, he was twice summoned to the White army, and twice he deserted. He did not want to take part in that civil war. His stepmother helped to solve the problem, making him the documents in the name of a native of the city of Lutsk, - at the time it was under Poland, and it was impossible to verify the authenticity of the documents.

In the 30's he moved to Siberia where mostly on his own funds he published his book "The Conquest of interplanetary space" which infuriated Russian officials as "absurd" and they sentenced him first to 3 years in GULAG, but then, as in case with Korolev 10 years later, changed it to "sharashka", the research institute of prison type.

Actually, Sergei Korolev before his own imprisonment wanted to obtain Kondratyuk as a theorist to his Jet Propulsion Study Group, but Kondratyuk declined.

Most likely Kondratyuk was right, or maybe it was just his premonition, but of the Group mentioned above, Korolev was one of the very few who survived the purges.

Korolev's arrest had a terrible effect on Kondratyuk - he immediately decided to get rid of his notes. But still believing in the good they can bring to humankind, he asked some reliable friend of his to take the notes and a copy of the book to the USA. The book will eventually find its way into the Library of Congress.

That is where the NASA engineer Houbolt will come across it sometime later.

Initially, there were three modes NASA considered for its trip to the Moon:

The first mode, called Direct Ascent, involved a single ship launching from Earth, landing on the moon and then returning to Earth. To go all the way fully intact, this ship would require huge amounts of fuel and be extremely technically complicated and massive.

The second method, Earth Orbit Rendezvous (EOR), foresaw two rockets launching into Earth orbit. One would carry the astronauts, the other fuel for the voyage. The two spacecraft would have to dock in Earth orbit and then head to the Moon. The single ship was to land on the Moon surface, astronauts do their work and then the spacecraft would lift off and return to Earth. EOR looked a bit better than the previous mode, but it would still require massive resources to launch two rockets and then carry basically two large ships to the Moon and back.

The third method, named Lunar Orbit Rendezvous (LOR), was the mode NASA engineer John Houbolt insisted on. It is the one Kondratyuk described in 1916. It foresaw sending one powerful rocket to the Moon's orbit with a detachable module, which would descend to the Moon's surface and then return to the Moon's orbit and dock with the main rocket.

NASA will eventually choose the LOR mode not knowing that Sergei Korolev had chosen it too already. He was building his N1 specifically for this type of flight.

Here are a couple of citations from the 1916-19 Kondratyuk's work "To Those Who Will Read in order to Build." It had existed only as a handwritten copy until it was finally published in 1964.

"It is obvious not to leave the whole rocket on the planet (Moon), but to launch it as a satellite (around the planet), and make a stop with the part of the rocket necessary for stopping on the planet and docking back with the vehicle. It is evident that using a small part of the rocket for landing makes it possible to save fuel and thus diminish the initial rocket mass approximately to one-half, according to the later calculations. Thus, currently, this scheme is the only possible solution"

"The rocket consists of a chamber where the passengers and the equipment are located and from which the vessels containing active substance are controlled. It also contains the tubes where the combustion of the active substance, as well as its expansion and that of its gases, takes place... Several vessels different in size should be made. Each vessel should have two compartments, for liquid oxygen and hydrogen."

Kondratyuk also independently derived the main equation for rocket motion.

Proved that a rocket has to drop fuel tanks to leave the boundaries of the Earth's gravity.

Described the scheme of a four-stage rocket;

Suggested using the gravity of the celestial bodies when calculating spacecraft trajectory. In great detail described modern-day spacesuits and Space stations.

Yuri Kondratyuk applied his talents on Earth as well. The most notable of them is the "Ostankino" TV station in Moscow. It was built after his death already by one of his students. The structure initially was created to be a giant Wind Power Plant which was to be mounted on top of Crimean highest mountain - Ai-Petri and was to produce 12,000 kilowatts. WPP project was fully approved but was closed because of the death of Sergo Ordzhonikidze, the head of People's Committee of Heavy Industry.

Yuri Kondratyuk (Aleksandr Sharhei) died in 1942 in the WW II battle near city Kirov.

Soviet authorities did not care much to commemorate Kondratyuk's achievements until Neil Armstrong's visit to USSR in 1970.

The American astronaut specifically went to Novosibirsk and took a handful of earth from the garden where Kondratyuk lived before going to the front.

After the event, a science center and college in Novosibirsk were given Kondratyuk's name. Streets in Poltava, Kiev, and Moscow started wearing his name. There is also the Kondratyuk crater on the Moon and a minor planet named after him.

In Independent Ukraine, Poltava Technical University wears Kondratyuk's name since 1997.

Yuri Kondratyuk was inducted into the International Space Hall of Fame in 2014.

Looking at how Russia treated the geniuses like Kalinin, Korolev, Kondratyuk, - torturing and imprisoning some, executing the others, forgetting their names, disrespecting their memories for long periods of times, - one wonders if there are inborn barbarian people exist, maybe there happen to be the whole groups or peoples as such even in our days?

Yuri Kondratyuk's 115th birthday anniversary celebrated by Google in 2012

Note of Interest.

While Kondratyuk calculations worked well to get the crew to the Moon, to get them back to the Moon orbit to their space station and back to the Earth, another formula was required. It was provided by

Dr. Ihor Bohachevsky, Professor of Mathematics at New York University. The formula was given his name and is known to the world as Bohachevsky Function. It is considered a benchmark test for the optimization algorithm.

Born in Western Ukraine in 1928, during WWII at the age 15, Ihor had to spend 2 years in German labor camp. In 1948 he moved to the USA and entered New York University in 1953 right after his return from the Korean War.

Apart from contributing to the success of the Apollo mission, Dr. Bohachevsky worked on issues connected with controlled inertial fusion process. He also worked as a mathematician at Bell Laboratories and Rocketdyne Division of Rockwell International where he was engaged in mathematical modeling of nuclear thermal rocket propulsion.

After 1991 he traveled to Ukraine often.

21.   Apollo, NRO, Comsat, GPS, Caribbean Crisis

One of the engineers laying the foundation of the Apollo systems in 1962 was Michael Yarymovych, born Mikhail Yarymovych in pre-WWII Ukraine. In his brief interview in 2014 to American Institute of Aeronautics and Astronautics (AIAA) after receiving Distinguished Service award for "60 years of dedicated service to IAS, ARS, AIAA and IAF, and for outstanding leadership for the aerospace profession in government, industry and the international community", Dr. Yarymovych recalled: "I joined the NASA Apollo team in Washington as Assistant Director of Flight Systems, defining the requirements for all the internal systems, such as power, navigation, and attitude control. At that time I was 29 years old, and so were most of my colleagues. Joe Shea was the "old man" at the age of 35." The moment when Joe Shea asked him to join his Systems Engineering team, Michael Yarymovych named as his absolute favorite in his entire long and eventful career.

So, Ukrainian intellect was helpful not just outside Apollo mission, but also within.

The Yarymovych family had to move to the United States because their native city of Ternopil was swept with WWII. It was young Mikhail's experience during the Berlin Airlift in 1948 that shaped his inspiration to become an airspace engineer: "I was growing up in post-war Berlin, Germany. During the Soviet blockade of the city, we were supplied food and fuel by the so-called Berlin Airlift. The DC-3s that were coming in four-minute intervals to Templehof airport were quite a sight for a 14-year-old boy, and especially the chocolates and candy that the U.S. Air Force pilots were dropping on approach and takeoff. Right then I decided to be an aeronautical engineer to design and build

121

these flying machines. Also, an old high school teacher gave me a book on astronomy, so I got excited about exploration of the stars." There was his father's influence also, because, as Yarymovych described in the same interview, his father was a mechanical engineer, so it must have been in the genes as well.

International Academy of Astronautics (IAA) presented Yarymovych with an award for his outstanding contributions to human space flight programs, such as Apollo and the Space Shuttle; for his role in the initiation of the global positioning system (GPS); and in the development of space launch vehicles.

Here is how "initiation of the GPS" looked in reality.

In 1973, Michael Yarymovych was appointed Chief Scientist of the US Air Force and was given a task to promote Defense Navigation Satellite System (DNSS). The problem was that there was a Navy system, Transit, but it provided accuracy within 83 feet and the vessel had to be almost stationary to use it.

Because of some misunderstandings between Air Force and Navy over certain issues, the same year DNSS was canceled, and it is only because of Yarymovych persistence the program was given the second chance. For this to happen, Yarymovych said he had to go on bended knees and plead – all because he had faith in the system and was confident it could benefit US Military tremendously.

Apart from finding compromises between Air Force, Navy, and Army, Michael Yarymovych managed to remove a psychological barrier in his audience by replacing a turnoff word "satellite" with the word "global."

That is how GPS term was coined. It will become fully operational only in 1994 but will exceed all the brightest expectations almost immediately. The fact that in less than 10 years during 2003 Operation Iraqi Freedom 70 percent of munitions dropped were guided mainly by GPS, speaks for itself. Even air refuelings were conducted with the help of GPS!

Actually, Yarymovych envisioned that in a short while almost all military systems would be dependent on GPS guidance, but even he was amazed by the ways and speed it spread in the civilian world. Agriculture, cars, phones, cartography, sport and even tectonics are some of the areas where GPS is used nowadays.

As for the ties with his historic homeland, Yarymovych became one of the creators of the Ukrainian Engineers' Society, helped found Ukrainian Research Institute at Harvard and supported other Ukrainian communities in the United States. After Ukraine received Independence in 1991, Dr. Yarymovych became a foreign member of the Academy of Science of Ukraine.

———

In the same position of a Chief Scientist of the US Air Force Michael Yarymovych was in the 80s, another Ukrainian, or, to be exact, Ukrainian-Canadian, briefly served in the year 1959 only to become the Undersecretary of the Airforce in 1960 and be appointed by the President Kennedy the first director of the National Reconnaissance Office in 1961. His name was Joseph Vincent Charyk.

Born in 1920, to Ukrainian immigrant parents John and Anna, Joseph was raised in a small red brick railway section house in Canmore, Canada, with his four siblings, John, Nick, Mary, and Helen.

The task of Charyk as the director of the National Reconnaissance Office was to consolidate C.I.A., Air Force, and Navy's space programs into one of the "Big Five" U.S. Intelligence agencies that would design, build and operate the reconnaissance satellites for the U.S. government.

It was to his expertise President John F. Kennedy called upon during the Cuban Missile Crisis to help interpret pictures and learn if there were in fact missiles on the ground in Cuba.

Ironically, Caribbean Crisis happened mostly because of technological breakthrough in missile building in Ukraine, the Charyks' historical homeland. The R-12 rockets were designed and engineered in Dnepropetrovsk's OKB-586, and became the first operationally effective intermediate range ballistic missiles, the first Soviet missiles deployed with a thermonuclear warhead, and the first mass-produced missiles in history. It is these missiles and their launchers on October 14, 1962, U-2 spy plane spotted in the western part of Cuba.

There were 24 launchers and 36 R-12 whose range of 1,292 miles could hit as far north as New York or as far west as Dallas.

In addition to that, there were to have been 16 launchers for R-14 whose larger range of 2,500 miles would make most of the US potential target. They were also produced in Ukraine, also had 1-megaton warheads, but did not make it to Cuba because of blockade. The ships carrying them turned around in the Atlantic on October 23.

A year later Kennedy would turn to Charyk again, appointing him to the founding board of an organization "formed to create and maintain a global network of commercial communications satellites", called Comsat. That is how Joseph Charyk became the technical expert responsible for the design of the actual satellite system and for the placement of satellites in synchronous orbits where they were to circle the earth at a rate of speed and altitude and keep each over a fixed point.

To make it work, Charyk had to fight skepticism that this complicated technology would not work even for voice transmission because of a half-second time delay. He also had to seek support and enlist the cooperation of other countries around the world, and even look for investors and customers for the quasi-private Communications Satellite Corp.

The task was accomplished making Joseph Charyk the founder of the geosynchronous communications satellite industry. In May 1965 Comsat became the first commercial venture to transmit live television programming across the Atlantic, thus forever changing the global communications industry.

Joseph Charyk also brought the first United States imagery satellite, Corona, into operation and demonstrated the space intelligence technology.

Charyk served as President, CEO, and Chairman at Comsat from 1963 to 1985.

In 1973 Joseph Vincent Charyk was inducted into the National Academy of Sciences and National Academy of Engineering for "basic contributions relating to space flight and leadership in the development of communications satellites".

In 1974 he received the International Emmy Directorate Award for his work with Comsat.

In 1987 President Ronald Reagan awarded Charyk the National Medal of Technology and Innovation "for employment of the concept of the geosynchronous communications satellite systems as the basis for a global telecommunications system, established by international agreement, and for his guidance in the development and growth of the Intelsat system, which today services over 150 nations and territories."

Dr. Joseph Charyk was also an honorary member of the Ukrainian Engineers Society of America.

22.   US Atomic Bomb, Cruise Missiles

George Bohdan Kistiakowsky was born November 18, 1900, in Kiev. His father Bohdan Kistiakowsky was Professor of Legal Philosophy at the University of Kiev and a member of the National Academy of Sciences of Ukraine.

When the Bolsheviks approached Kiev in 1918, George Kistiakowsky joined White Army and fought in infantry and tank corps. After the Bolshevik victory, Kistiakowsky fled to Germany, where he began to study at the University of Berlin in 1921.

"As a woefully unprepared student, I was admitted in 1921 to the University of Berlin after years of soldering in Ukraine and then living by manual labor in the Balkans. Somewhat later I started attending the Physics Colloquium, the like of which probably will never happen again. Led by Einstein and Planck, the whole contingent of senior physicists assembled there", recalled George Kistiakowsky the events of those days in the 1982 Bulletin of the Atomic Scientists.

He received a Ph.D. in chemistry in 1925, then moved to the United States the next year and taught at Princeton as an International Education Board Fellow. He also taught at Harvard University, where he became Professor of Chemistry in 1938.

It is while teaching at Harvard throughout the 1940s, Kistiakowsky started to apply his expertise in thermodynamics, spectroscopy, and chemical kinetics to military research. So it was no surprise that the US Government called on Dr. Kistiakowsky to help solve the problem with the new weapon physicists at Los Alamos had been struggling for some time already with – they could not create an implosion capable of igniting the atomic bomb's plutonium core.

George Kistiakowsky joined the Manhattan Project in 1944, replacing Seth Neddermeyer as head of the Explosives ("X") Division for the National Defense Research Committee responsible for the explosive components of fission weapons. It is under his leadership the complex explosive lenses capable to compress the plutonium sphere to achieve critical mass were developed.

Actually, as an American journalist and historian Richard Rhodes writes in his Pulitzer Prize-winning book *The Making of the Atomic Bomb*, George Kistiakowsky turned out to be a key figure in the whole Manhattan Project. Especially its practical part.

- It was Kistiakowsky's judgment that convinced the chairman of the National Defense Research Committee (NDRC) James B. Conant who was very skeptical in the beginning. Conant knew Kistiakowsky well because it was he, already a Harvard President at the age of 40, had lured Kiev-born specialist from Princeton. "My doubts about Briggs' project evaporated as soon as I heard George Kistiakowsky's verdict," will write Conant in his memoirs later.

- The implosives was the only real hope for the Trinity Device to work, but it was so hard to make, that at one time Robert Oppenheimer considered resigning his directorship because of it. Kistiakowsky recalled: "so much pessimism was developing about our ability to build satisfactory lenses, that Captain Parsons began urging (and he was not alone in this) that we give up lenses completely and try somehow to patch up non-lens type of implosion."

- Kistiakowsky introduced the most dramatic innovation of finishing the high-explosive castings by machining them.

- In February 1945, Kistiakowsky chose an explosive called Composition B to serve as the fast-burning component of Fat Man's lenses. It had to be poured as a hot slurry of wax, molten TNT and other components and then cooled in certain ways to avoid air bubbles inside the large castings fifty pounds and more each. "The explosive was poured in and then people sat over that damned thing watching it as if it was egg being hatched, changing the temperature of the water running through the various cooling tubes built into the mold." Because of Kistiakowsky's precision approach, there was not a single explosive accident in over 50,000 machining operations on those castings.

- On April 11, 1945, Oppenheimer sent Groves the news that Kistiakowsky had managed to produce implosive compressions so perfectly symmetrical that their numbers agreed with theoretical prediction.

- Truman postponed the conference with Stalin and Churchill in Potsdam until July 15 on purpose to give the Los Alamos team more time. To make sure the President had news of the test during the conference, the test date was set on July 16. Successful test of the atomic bomb would be a substitute for Soviet entry into the Pacific war.

- By July, the pace of the whole test depended on the delivery of full-time molds for the implosion lens segments and Kistiakowsky's group worked night and day to make them. The problem was that the air cavities in the interior of the castings produced too many rejects. The team was able to detect the cavities by x-ray, but could not repair them.

- July 9 Kistiakowsky, "in some desperation", got hold of a dental drill and, not wishing to ask others to do a dangerous job, spent most of the night, the week before the Trinity test, drilling holes in the faulty castings as to reach the air cavities. "You do not worry about it," he will comment later, "I mean, if fifty pounds of explosives goes in your lap, you won't know it."

- The same day, the Creutz group fired the Chinese copy, measured the simultaneity of its implosion by the magnetic method and made a conclusion that Trinity bomb was likely to fail. "So of course," Kistiakowsky recalls, "I immediately became the chief villain and everybody lectured me...Everybody at the headquarters became terribly upset and focused on my presumed guilt. Oppenheimer, General Groves, Vannevar Bush – all had much to say about that incompetent wretch who forever after would be known to the world as the cause of the tragic failure of the Manhattan Project... At another point Oppenheimer became so emotional that I offered him a month's salary against ten dollars that our implosion charge would work."

- Early morning July 16, the day of the test, Kistiakowsky found the control post rather crowded, "and having now nothing to do, I left as soon as the automatic timer was thrown in... and went to stand on the earth mound covering the concrete dugout. (My own guess was that the yield would be about 1 kiloton, and so five miles seemed very safe." The blast knocked him down at S-10000. He scrambled up, watched the fireball rise, mushroom auras, and moved back to the control panel. "I slapped Oppenheimer on the back and said, 'Oppie, you owe me ten dollars.' "The distracted Los Alamos director searched his wallet. "It's empty," he told Kistiakowsky, "you'll have to wait."

How important was that achievement?

George Marshall, American Secretary of State and Secretary of Defense under Truman, said after the war: "We regarded the matter of dropping the atomic bomb as exceedingly important. We had just gone through a bitter experience at Okinawa (the last major island campaign, when the Americans lost more than 12,500 men killed and missing and the Japanese more than 100,000 killed in eighty-two days of fighting). This had been preceded by a number of similar experiences in other Pacific islands, north of Australia. The Japanese had demonstrated in each case they would not surrender and they would fight to the death… It was expected that resistance in Japan, with their home ties, would be even more severe. We had had the 100,000 people killed in Tokyo in one night of conventional bombs, and it had had seemingly no effect whatsoever. It destroyed the Japanese cities, yes, but their morale was not affected as far as we could tell, not at all. So, it seemed quite necessary, if we could, to shock them into action… We had to end the war; we had to save American lives."

"Stimson argued that because of the mountainous Japanese terrain and because "the Japanese are highly patriotic and certainly susceptible to calls for fanatical resistance to repel an invasion," America would probably "have to go through with even more bitter finish fight than in Germany" if it attempted to invade."

"To avert a vast, indefinite butchery," Winston Churchill summarizes in his history of the Second World War, "to bring the war to an end, to give peace to the world, to lay healing hands upon its tortured peoples by a manifestation of overwhelming power at the cost of a few explosions, seemed, after all our toils and perils, a miracle of deliverance."

In terms of saving lives in this perspective, George Kistiakowsky's input can hardly be overestimated. Especially taken into account the fact that, according to Richard Rhodes, "it was Kistiakowsky who explained the great economic advantage of being able to deliver a heavy blow with a bomb carried by a single plane."

After World War II, Kistiakowsky returned to teach at Harvard.

Apart from his academic work, George Kistiakowsky often advised the Federal Government. In 1959, he became a Science Adviser to President Dwight D. Eisenhower, and in 1961 - a member of the United States Arms Control and Disarmament Agency.

Physical chemist; member of the National Academy of Sciences of the United States and vice-president of it in the years 1965–71,he was also a full member of the Shevchenko Scientific Society.

Dr. Kistiakowsky was awarded the Medal of Merit by President Truman, the Medal of Freedom by President Eisenhower in 1961, and the National Medal of Science by President Lyndon Johnson in 1967. He also published a great number of scientific works mainly in the areas of chemical kinetics, thermodynamics of organic molecules, and shock and detonation.

———————

Another Ukraine-born engineer helped create American cruise missiles.

Dr. Bohdan T. Hnatiuk worked as a consultant for the Bendix Aviation Corporation, Guided Missile Section, on the U.S. Navy Talos Project (1955-1957). He was a consultant to the U.S. Navy's Allegheny Ballistic Laboratory and to Pneumo-Dynamic Corp. in Washington. In 1967-1969 Dr. Bohdan Hnatiuk took part in space research for NASA at the Alabama - George C. Marshall Space Flight Center.

One wonders if it is just a coincidence that one of the best American cruise missiles wears the same name as a national symbol and Coat of Arms of not just Ukraine, but of the Kiev Rus also – Trident?

23.   Elon Musk's Favorite non-SpaceX Rocket

In May 2015 during CNN's Rapid Fire blitz interview, SpaceX founder said that his favorite non-SpaceX rocket was Ukrainian Zenith.

It was interesting to read the educated discussion on the SpaceX subReddit devoted to this case. The major question of course was - are there any similarities between Zenith and Falcon? The most popular comment turned out to have become this one:

"A lot of similarities! Both the Falcon 9 and Zenit are two-stage, kerosene/LOX rockets that can put about 13 tons into LEO or 5 tons to GTO. They're pretty similar in overall size - Falcon a bit taller and skinnier.

The RD-120 upper stage engine on the Zenit is roughly comparable to the Merlin -- it's a bit bigger as well as slightly more efficient because of its staged combustion cycle as opposed to Merlin's open cycle gas generator driven pump system.

Zenit's first-stage RD-171 is a 4-chamber, 4-nozzle, single-turbopump system, a little more powerful than the 9-Merlin cluster, and again, more efficient due to its staged combustion cycle.

Interestingly, SpaceX's Raptor engine is supposed to be staged-combustion."

Zenith Space Launch Vehicle is produced in the city of Dnipro (former Dnipropetrovsk), Ukraine at Yuzhnoe Plant.

The official site of the plant says that there have been 876 successful launches of Zenith vehicle already and probably it's one of the main features that made this rocket stand out for the current Space Entrepreneur #1 in the world.

Zenith is also the rocket used in the Sea Launch Project.

What was also revealing is that after the successful launch of his Falcon Heavy in February 2018, in one of his interviews Elon Musk mentioned the heavy N-1 rocket. The one described briefly above and tied with Sergei Korolev. The one that failed 4 times after Korolev's death.

Falcon Heavy was designed to deliver a payload of 64 tons to a low-Earth orbit, just like N-1.

And in the interview, SpaceX founder said that he understands where in his opinion there was a problem with the N-1. He assured that all the measures have been taken for his Falcon Heavy with 27 engines not to suffer the fate of the 30 engine N-1.

"I think with the N-1 failure it was mostly avionics failure. They had engine fire issues," he said.

These two cases of Zenith and N-1 demonstrate that Mr. Musk does a thorough study of the outstanding rockets engineered even decades ago.

As a matter of fact, to deliver some outsized parts for Falcon Heavy launch, SpaceX had to turn to Ukrainian AN-124 "Ruslan". This plane was hugely advertised by the recent Mega Machine documentary on Science Channel.

Note of Interest. Some readers may be interested to learn that there is a significant Ukrainian input in the Antares project. Namely, the first stage core structure was designed and manufactured in the same city of Dnipro mentioned earlier. There were also companies in the cities like Kiev, Chernihiv and Kharkiv which participate in the project.

24. SS-18 "Satan" ICBM, Canadian Launch Pad

It is the world's largest and most dangerous Intercontinental Ballistic Missile (ICBM) ever built.

Solely Ukraine's know-how.

Highly accurate guided missile housed in silos.

The works started in 1962 in the Ukrainian city of Dnipro (former Dnipropetrovsk) and the first rockets were tested in 1970.

The later version, the R-36M, received NATO reporting name SS-18 Satan.

The final (Mod-6) modification, R-36M-2 "Voevoda" deployed in August 1988 could deliver 18–20 Megaton (Mt) warhead at a distance of 16,000 km., making it the heaviest and the world's longest-range missile.

Its liquid rocket engines provide a speed of about 7.9km/sec. and make it possible to reach American continent in roughly 20 minutes.

Majority of military experts view this rocket as the most dangerous of all in the world - its characteristics included rapid silo-reload ability, extra heavy throw weight and very large number of re-entry vehicles. Some versions of the R-36M were armed with 10 warheads and up to 40 penetration aids.

The 10 independent, 750 kiloton nuclear warheads, each had more than 40 times the destructive power of the bomb that destroyed Hiroshima.

For comparison, the US contemporary rival to R-36M, such as the Minuteman III, could carry up to three warheads at most at the time.

The American administrations in the 80s and 90s made the Ukraine-engineered missiles the main focus of their arms control initiatives. The START II Treaty (Strategic Arms Reduction Treaty) specifically foresaw banning land-based Multiple Independently Targetable Reentry Vehicles (MIRV) systems, mostly because of the threat the SS-18 posed to the balance of power.

Since SS-18 was Ukraine's know-how, it was only Ukraine, who produced and serviced these rockets for the whole Soviet Union.

When the Soviet Union disintegrated and Ukraine signed the Budapest Memorandum, it stopped producing these rockets but continued to service the ones in Russia's arsenal.

With the start of Russia's aggression against Ukraine, Ukraine quit even up keeping the rockets which still constitute very significant part of Russia's nuclear shield.

As of now, according to the Jamestown Foundation, "Russian ICBMs: An Aging but Mixed Arsenal" publication as of October 25, 2017, there are 46 SS-18 Satan missiles left in Russia, and Russian facility cannot cope with up keeping them without access to the missile's design documentation stored in Ukraine.

Russia tries hard to replace the R-36M with its new heavy ICBM, the RS-28 Sarmat. So far, this missile dubbed by NATO "SS-X-30" "Satan-2" has seen numerous delays.

It is this very nuclear missile Putin tried to scare the USA with during his public address March 1, 2018, but made a laughing matter of himself by showing 10-year-old clip with animation about Ukrainian Voevoda mentioned above.

According to the Foundation article above, Moscow also has 40 SS-19 Stiletto missiles similar to SS-18, "but the guidance system was built by factories now found in independent Ukraine."

Russia's Strategic Rocket Forces "could decline to 35 percent by around 2020, if the older ICBMs in the inventory cannot be kept operational," - the article concludes.

In short, without Ukraine, Russia's nuclear arsenal is in trouble.

Bad for Russia, good for the civilized world.

Safer for the United States, since the SS-18 rockets are Intercontinental, meaning they were specifically designed to reach other continents.

As for Ukraine and its unique technologies in designing the scariest weapon of modern war, they will be used for the good of humanity now.

Actually, this rocket, the SS-18 some 19 years ago was already used for civilian purposes - in the year 1999, it was launched from a silo at the Baikonur Cosmodrome in Kazakhstan under the name of Dnepr-1 (named after the river Dnieper). It did a perfect job placing an Earth observation satellite built by the UK company into a low, 650km orbit.

To the surprise of many, Canada is currently building a launch pad specifically for the Ukrainian rocket - Cyclone-4M.

And you know what? Cyclone-4M is basically the same RD-36M/ SS-18. The same Dnepr-1.

The project is being run by the Maritime Launch Services and here is what they have to say:

"This is a fully commercial endeavor based on no government funding. The reason we can do this for a modest $226 million is because we are basing it on so much capability, and so many existing designs, from Ukraine. We don't have to design things from scratch.

In other words, American aerospace entrepreneurs will be using Ukrainian rockets to launch satellites from around the world from a spaceport in eastern Canada. This beautifully encapsulates the increasingly interlinked network of rocket-makers, launch providers, and emerging commercial satellite markets that underpins the modern space sector."

First launches are scheduled for 2019 already with minimum 8 launches annually from then on.

A proposal has also recently been made to modify SS-18 Satan ICBMs and use them to destroy incoming asteroids of up to 100 m in diameter threatening the Earth.

No more need for Bruce Willis dying preventing Armageddon, huh? Thanks to Ukraine.

Note of Interest. There is a unique Strategic Missile Forces Museum in Ukraine not far from Kiev. It also hosts Unified Launch Control Center, which is situated 12 floors below the ground.

The base housed nuclear missile operations until the site was decommissioned in the 1990s. Until then, the base had 86 intercontinental ballistic missiles with one fully dismantled on display there.

This base is in Pervomaysk, Ukraine – about a four-hour drive from Kiev.

In 1994, three years after Ukraine became independent, it joined the Non-Proliferation Treaty and agreed to dismantle its 1,900 Soviet missiles. At the time, Ukraine boasted the world's third-largest stockpile of nuclear warheads after Russia and the United States. Ukraine shipped its nuclear warheads to Russia and dismantled its silos, often blowing them up or filling them with cement. The control silo at Pervomaysk was the only one spared – so it could become a museum.

25.   "Russian Woodpecker". Chernobyl

In July 1976, shortwave radios throughout the world, the United States including, started picking up signals in the 4 to 30 MHz range. Signals were so powerful that even commercial airliners and telephone circuits started having difficulties in communication.

Conspiracy theories surrounding the notorious signals ranged from Soviet mind control to weather experiments, including sabotage of western broadcast and submarine communications.

But when the survey showed that Soviet stations were as badly affected by the interference as Western stations, the broadcast theory was debunked.

Because the signal was a sharp set of pulses, usually ten, but sometimes up to twenty per second and was reminiscent of a woodpecker when played over a speaker, it was dubbed accordingly as the Russian Woodpecker. It was called Russian since amateur radio enthusiast established the source to be in the region of the former USSR where Ukraine, Belarus, and Russia meet.

NATO had its own name for the source of the signal - "Steel Yard".

The name was not accidental since in reality it turned out to be an immense structure of metal girders and wires, taller than the Sydney Harbour Bridge or Egyptian Pyramids at 146 meters and stretching more than 500 meters wide.

This huge rectangular stood not far from the then-obscure Chernobyl nuclear plant.

Yes, the notorious Russian Woodpecker was, and still is some 10 miles away from the now-closed Chernobyl nuclear station and the secret city where the operating staff of the station lived was called Chernobyl-2.

Duga (that was its real name meaning "Arc" in English) was Over-The-Horizon (OTH) radar system used as part of the Soviet Anti-Ballistic-Missile (ABM) early-warning network.

There were 4 radars in the whole Soviet Union, with 3 of them being in Ukraine and 1 - in Siberia.

Experimental and the first Duga-1 was built outside Mykolaiv in Ukraine and successfully detected rocket launches from Baikonur Cosmodrome at 2,500 kilometers.

Duga-2 was built on the same site and proved capable of tracking launches from the Far East and submarines in the Pacific Ocean. Both Duga 1 and 2 were aimed east and were of fairly low power.

The idea of building these two "trial" Dugas near Mykolaiv is most likely connected with the fact that Mykolaiv was the only plant in the former USSR deep and equipped enough to build aircraft carriers. Current Russian "Admiral Kuznetsov" and China's "Liaoning" flagman aircraft carriers were built in Mykolaiv.

Duga-3, the one near Chernobyl, the Woodpecker #1 pointed north-northwest, the direction from which an American nuclear strike was expected.

It is the one which caused all the inconveniences to the point that some receivers such as amateur radios and televisions actually began including 'Woodpecker Blankets' in their design.

And it was near nuclear power plant for a reason - due to its high power demands.

"If anything, the military purpose of Chernobyl-2 (Woodpecker's closed zone) is a reminder that the purpose of the Chernobyl power station was never entirely civilian, either. While it did provide vast amounts of electricity to Ukraine, its four reactors were of the RBMK variety (graphite-moderated nuclear High Power Channel-type Reactor), meaning they could be easily switched between the fission of uranium for civilian purposes and the enrichment of plutonium for military ones. That left the top of reactor lightly covered, in order to make the switching of fuel assemblies easier. That's why, when the thing unleashed its fiery belch one April day, a good part of Europe got a dusting of radionuclides," tells its readers the Newsweek article "The Massive Russian Radar Site in the Chernobyl Exclusion Zone."

Duga-4, Woodpecker #2 was built near Komsomolsk-Na-Amure (near the Amur River in Siberia). It was positioned to give coverage to Alaska and the West coast of the United States.

After the Chernobyl meltdown, the movable equipment of the "Ukrainian Woodpecker" was shipped off to the "Siberian" one. In 1989 it also was decommissioned - there was no use of the second one without the first one.

Conspiracy Theory. In the year 2015, a documentary film by Chad Garcia "Russian Woodpecker" was released.

In the beginning, it is quite bizarre and when the authors voice a conspiracy theory that Chernobyl's disaster was hand-made to cover the defects in the Woodpecker's design, one starts thinking that it's not funny.

Then, when the costs of building the OTH radar are given, and it turns out to be 7 billion rubles, which was almost the same amount in dollars, and which is roughly 3 times more than the cost of building Chernobyl nuclear plant itself, the attention sharpens.

The final evaluation of the Woodpecker was set for September of 1986, but it had become evident earlier that it would fail it for the reason of Aurora Borealis, or Northern Light which was blocking the signal.

If such a multi-billion miscalculation was to be discovered, someone high-ranked in Moscow responsible for the project would have lost not just his position, but, most likely his life too.

Some interviews in the film confirm that during the workers' late shits that tragic night of meltdown, there were calls from Moscow ordering to continue dangerous experiment knowing well that it may end in disaster.

The authors of the film name that man, who they think responsible – he happened to be the Minister of Communications and a Vice President of the Soviet-Cuban Friendship Society.

The film became Grand Jury Prize Winner at Sundance Film Festival, meaning some people found it at least worth watching.

Conspiracy theory #2

Another conspiracy theory derives from the state the USSR was at the time. The war in Afghanistan had been dragging for 6 years already consuming vast resources, In the first half of 1986 crude oil prices fell to about $12 a barrel. European countries were considering building more nuclear power plants.

Below are some excerpts from the world press after the Chernobyl meltdown:

"If the blow to nuclear energy is as severe as the securities markets fear, the result could be upward pressure on prices of oil as well as natural gas and coal. A rise in energy prices could wipe out a key factor that has been pushing down the rate of inflation in the United States and the global economy." – *NY Times* on May 02, 1986.

"The 1986 Chernobyl disaster, the world's biggest nuclear accident, turned Germans against atomic energy for years as they panicked about safety and the environment, fears the Green lobby capitalized on to strengthen their influence." – *Reuters*.

"The data demonstrates its impact: in the 32 years before Chernobyl, 409 reactors were opened, but only 194 have been connected in the three decades since." – *The Guardian*.

"The accident couldn't have happened at a worse time. The Berlin Wall came crashing down in 1990, ending the Soviet Union. Both Ukraine and Belarus had been former U.S.S.R. satellite countries. Now, they were facing independence. Ukraine had been the "breadbasket" of the Soviet world. The accident destroyed this role. There were few small businesses to take its place. The accident made new business development more difficult. Few companies wanted to invest in an area threatened by radiation. Who wants to buy a product marked "Made in Chernobyl"?" – *The Balance*.

Is it possible Chernobyl disaster was used by Moscow to try to raise the oil and gas prices for the long run by averting people from the nuclear energy and to keep Europe and Russia's "satellite countries" such as Ukraine and Belarus in its sphere of influence?

26. Chernobyl firefighters, Dr. Gale, Kiev Medical Miracle

After the Chernobyl HBO miniseries had been televised, another side of the drama was rediscovered in Ukraine. Everyone who watched the show most likely remembers the firefighters crew and their treatment in Moscow. In reality, it was only part of that crew who were transported to Moscow. They were considered lucky at the time because they were taken to hospital #6 which was the only specialized hospital in the whole USSR to treat the patient with radiation diseases.

Now it has become known that the hospital during the first several weeks relied heavily on the instructions of an American doctor who insisted on bone marrow transplants. His name was Dr. Robert Gale.

In 1988, *Los Angeles Times* published an article "Chernobyl 'Hero': Dr. Gale --"Medical Maverick."

"As the physician who led the international "rescue team" that helped treat victims of the Chernobyl nuclear plant accident, Gale has been a darling of the news media for two years. He has been interviewed by Barbara Walters, made guest appearances on the "Donahue" and Larry King shows and been featured in Time, Life, Vanity Fair--even Pravda--to name a few.

Yet there is something about the Chernobyl effort that is not mentioned in Gale's book nor in the numerous interviews he has given since the summer of 1986. According to documents recently obtained by The Times, Gale designed and helped carry out experimental treatments on at least three Soviet citizens with a genetically engineered drug that had never before been tried on human subjects, nor approved for human testing."

LA Times proceeds to tell that Gale's primary interest was in cancer of the blood or cancer of the bone marrow.

When Gale heard a news report about a serious accident at a Soviet nuclear power plant north of Kiev, he was confident that those people from Chernobyl may need bone marrow transplants and his help too.

"In all, according to Soviet physicians, only 13 bone marrow transplants and six fetal liver cell transplant operations were done and some of them were completed before Gale and his colleagues even arrived. But Gorbachev had thanked Gale personally and the Soviet doctors invited him back.

In a report issued the summer after the Chernobyl accident, Soviet medical authorities concluded that the bone marrow transplants turned out to have little practical value and probably hastened the death of at least two patients. In future nuclear accidents, the Soviet doctors concluded, bone marrow transplants would benefit only a small number of patients exposed to a narrow range of radiation doses."

Soviet media provided a different number of bone marrow transplants though. In his interview to Novosti News Agency on May 20, 1986, Anrey Ivanovich Vorobyev, corresponding member of the USSR Academy of Medical Sciences said the following:

"[Question] American specialists — in particular, Professors Gale and Tarasaki — have come to Moscow. What necessitated this?

[Answer] Under ordinary conditions, physicians around the world resort to bone marrow transplants infrequently — there are many unresolved problems in this procedure. But now there has arisen the need for bone marrow transplants immediately for many patients... Professor Gale is a leading specialist on bone marrow transplants in the United States. Professor Tarasaki is the originator of unique methodologies for titration — the determination of the degree of compatibility of bone marrow tissue. The bone marrow of the donor must be as compatible as possible, in order not to cause the organism to reject it, as any other foreign substance. In a word, bone-marrow transplants are a very difficult job. They have been carried out on 19 patients who required the procedure."

Later on, in *Radiobiology for the Radiologist,* there was a more profound summary: "Only the patients in Moscow received bone marrow transplants. Out of these 2 survived, and only 1 showed autologous bone marrow re-population (and even that result is questionable). The use of bone marrow transplantation sounds obvious at first sight (which is why it has been attempted, not only with Chernobyl but other accidents as well). However, very little success has been had with them. The problem is that there is a very small window of dose where a bone marrow transplant might be beneficial."

What the Moscow doctors discovered afterward, the Kiev medics seem to have figured out immediately. Anna Gubareva, an oncologist at the Institute of Radiology and Oncology in Kiev recalls the first days after Chernobyl meltdown: "Our professor, Leonid Kindzelskiy, was the chief radiologist of Ukraine. I was then a graduate student in the Department of Systemic Tumor Diseases and was just starting my postgraduate studies at what is now the Cancer Institute.

When I came to the meeting, there was an almost military situation in the Institute: the first groups of explosion victims arrived on April 27. Leonid Kindzelskiy with other doctors equipped with dosimetrists went to the Chernobyl nuclear power station; they selected patients with radiation sickness symptoms. At least 191 people arrived at our institute; now nobody knows the exact number, because all the medical records were taken by the KGB. It was secret information; we were forced to sign a non-disclosure document.

Leonid Kindzelskiy had his own ideas on how to treat the victims. It was immediately clear that there is not only gamma-radiation but also radioactive isotopes. People inhaled all that, it was on their skin. We changed their clothes, washed their skin, gave them infusions for a whole day. We did not have enough pajamas for all patients; we dressed them in women's shirts, in women's dressing gowns. Of course, those clothes did not fit, because firefighters and workers were physically strong men. When the blood tests of liquidators were getting worse, we transmitted bone marrow to them. Almost all the patients we had in the Institute survived."

The difference in treatments appears to be the following: in Moscow, they "killed" the bone morrow of the firefighters and then waited for the one from a donor to adapt, while in Kiev they did not "kill" the patient's morrow, but were "planting in" the donor one intravenously.

"In the early days, it was difficult. The physicians and nurses in the department, among them physician B.M. Baydman, lay on tables giving their own blood for direct transfusion to the people stricken with radiation. "

To the possible questions of whether the Moscow part of the firefighters' crew might have received a higher radiation dosage, here is a story from a reporter for Moscow's *Literaturnaya Gazeta* from Kiev in August 1986: "Firefighter Leonid Shavrey from the already legendary subdivision of Lieutenant V. Pravik, stayed at his post that night on the roof of the reactor to stop the fire from spreading further. He was really hot; he even tossed his helmet aside at one point. The night was just a night, the fire just a fire; he noticed nothing supernatural. It was only when he came down that the taste of a cigarette suddenly seemed sweetly nauseating... "

Anyone who watched the miniseries or read about Chernobyl can understand what being on the roof of the reactor even for a brief time meant.

But still, how was it decided who goes to Moscow and who goes to Kiev? Did the patients spend days in some local clinic where the doctors determined the degree of radiation received?

Ukrainian writer, doctor of medical science Yuriy Shcherbak writes: "It is no easy thing to leaf through the case history of those who, fearing neither fire nor radiation, dashed to the reactor in order to save all of us from the catastrophe that threatened us. Those patients did not stay long in Polesskiy (hospital) — only a few hours (they were sent by air to Moscow for treatment), but the medics will remember them for the rest of their lives."

This short excerpt shows that the patients who the medics delivered to the Polesskiy hospital, which is situated some 50 kilometers to the west from Chernobyl, were sent to Moscow within just several hours by helicopters. The other firemen from the same crew working in the very same conditions and even on the roof of the reactor like Ivan Shavrey, the medics rushed south to Kiev which is only 100 kilometers away.

Here is another powerful story the reporter tells: "Firetruck driver from Chernobyl, Grigoriy Matveyevich Khmel, the senior of all these boys now charging about in the section or watching television, was wistfully looking through the window beyond which the unprecedentedly beautiful Ukrainian springtime was unfolding. Grigoriy Matveyevich is a veteran old enough to remember the Great Patriotic War and bring up two sons, Petr and Ivan. The two sons are also firefighters, and that night they too fought the fire and the radiation, just like their papa; now they are receiving medical treatment: Petr in Moscow, Ivan in Kiev. Their mother has been evacuated from a village near Pripyat and is working in Borodyanskiy rayon, where she prepares food and takes it to the vehicle operators in the field. She is very busy and so she comes infrequently. Khmel talks with his sons on the telephone. "

"We are walking in the department with Professor L.P. Kindzelskiy, the chief radiologist of the Ukrainian SSR Ministry of Health and the scientific leader in this clinic. We stop in front of the glass-partitioned resuscitation rooms, filled with complicated equipment. We are silent, our heads bowed in sorrow. It was here that Aleksandr Grigoryevich Lelechenko died; his exploit is today known throughout the country. Lelechenko is a tender Ukrainian word that means child of the leleka —the stork. It was here that he folded his wings. The physicians were powerless. The others survived, and today

149

they feel much better. Some patients are nearly ready to be discharged."

The National Interest article of 2019 describes what Lelechenko did: "Ordering younger workers to stand down, 47-year-old electrician Aleksandr Lelechenko repeatedly ventured into the irradiated electrolysis room in an attempt to effect emergency repairs. He absorbed enough radiation to kill five men but, after receiving first aid at the clinic in Pripyat, he rushed back to Chernobyl to work.

Lelechenko returned home to have dinner with his wife that night, caught a few hours of sleep then — you guessed it — went back to Chernobyl again. "We have to save the station," he told his wife. He died two weeks later at a hospital in Kiev."

The moral of this chapter is no way to blame the American doctor – he did what he thought would save lives in those extraordinary circumstances. It is more about the gist of the huge nuclear country that had just one specialized hospital. It is even more about Kiev specialists who defied the system and saved lives.

Kiev doctors on the way to Chernobyl April 27, 1986

27. "Chicken Kiev Speech" by George H.W. Bush

"This beautiful city brings to mind the words of the poet Alexander Dovzhenko: "The city of Kiev is an orchard. Kiev is a poet. Kiev is an epic. Kiev is history. Kiev is art."

Centuries ago, your forebears named this country Ukraine, or "frontier," because your steppes link Europe and Asia. But Ukrainians have become frontiersmen of another sort. Today you explore the frontiers and contours of liberty." that is how the US President's speech in Ukrainian Parliament started August 1st, 1991. It was the first time ever an American President was giving a speech in those walls.

Beautiful words! So true!

"We will maintain the strongest possible relationship with the Soviet Government of President Gorbachev. But we also appreciate the new realities of life in the U.S.S.R. And therefore, as a federation ourselves, we want good relations -- improved relations -- with the Republics. So, let me build upon my comments in Moscow by describing in more detail what Americans mean when we talk about freedom, democracy, and economic liberty...

...Yet freedom is not the same as independence. Americans will not support those who seek independence in order to replace a far-off tyranny with a local despotism. They will not aid those who promote a suicidal nationalism based upon ethnic hatred."

So, freedom for Ukraine is not independence from Moscow?

Where did phrases about "ethnic hatred", "local despotism", and "suicidal nationalism" come from?

By a History provision, there were two people present and listening to what was being said during that speech..

The first one was William Safire, a political columnist for the New York Times.

Couple months later, he will publish an essay in the newspaper titled "Ukraine Marches On" where for the first time he will use the phrase "Chicken Kiev Speech" which will become proverbial:

"Unprincipled" is the word used to describe President Bush by Mykhailo Horyn, a former political prisoner, and founder of Rukh, the Ukrainian independence movement. "We prefer Thomas Jefferson."

Fighters for Ukraine free of Russian imperial rule are still smarting at Mr. Bush's speech in Kiev this summer blasting "suicidal nationalism" and touting the Gorbachev center.

That misreading of the forces of history in his "chicken Kiev" speech not only made one American President appear to be anti-liberty, but jeopardized our relations with an emerging European power.

Ukraine (the article "the" is dropped when referring to a country, not a province) is the great, hobnailed boot that will drop on Dec. 1 on top of Moscow center's pretensions to empire. On that day of the referendum, at least two out of three Ukrainians are likely to vote to assert their country's national sovereignty. On that day, the Soviet "union" will die."

If one has ever wondered if one person, one journalist would prove right where the whole US President Administration turn wrong, that was the perfect example – Ukraine did just as Mr. Safire predicted - it did drop the boot on Moscow's inflated ambitions that very year.

Alas, it did not end then for Ukraine.

13 years later, during the peaceful Orange Revolution in Ukraine, William Safire revealed some insights into how the article above affected his relationship with George H.W. Bush. This time the article in the NY Times was titled "Putin's Chicken Kiev":

"The elder President Bush's most memorable foreign-policy blunder took place in Kiev in 1991, then under Communist rule. With the Soviet Union coming apart, the U.S. president -- badly advised by the stability-obsessed "realist" Brent Scowcroft -- made a speech urging Ukrainians yearning for independence to beware of "suicidal nationalism." His speech, which he now insists meant only "not so fast," was widely taken as advice to remain loyal to Moscow's empire.

I dubbed this the "Chicken Kiev" speech. That so infuriated Bush, who mistakenly saw the phrase as imputing cowardice rather than charging colossal misjudgment that he has not spoken to me since."

Well, that speech may have affected the destiny of the elder President Bush himself.

The second person present in the Ukrainian Parliament during the speech was a young Canadian reporter of Ukrainian origin.

In less than 10 years she will become the bureau chief for the Financial Times in Moscow.

In another 10 years - Canada's Minister of Trade, and eventually in 2016 - Canada's Minister of Foreign Affairs.

Because of her stance and articles like "My Ukraine and Putin's Big Lies" she is a "persona non-grata" in Russia even in her current position as Canada's Minister of Foreign Affairs.

Her name was and is Ms. Christya Freeland.

In the article mentioned above, "My Ukraine", first published in Brookings in 2015, Ms. Freeland describes the situation with the speech at a distance of almost quarter of the century and the way she saw it:

""In July of that year 1991, Bush traveled first to Moscow to shore up Gorbachev, then to Ukraine, where, on Aug. 1, he delivered a speech to the Ukrainian Parliament exhorting his audience to give Gorbachev a chance at keeping the reforming Soviet Union together: "Americans will not support those who seek independence in order to replace a far-off tyranny with a local despotism. They will not aid those who promote a suicidal nationalism based upon ethnic hatred."

I was living in Kyiv at the time, working as a stringer for the FT, The Economist, and The Washington Post. Listening to Bush in the parliamentary press gallery, I felt he had misread the growing consensus in Ukraine. That became even clearer immediately afterward when I interviewed Ukrainian members of Parliament (MPs), all of whom expressed outrage and scorn at Bush for, as they saw it, taking Gorbachev's side. The address, which New York Times columnist William Safire memorably dubbed the "Chicken Kiev speech," backfired in the United States as well, antagonizing Americans of Ukrainian descent and other East European diasporas, which may have hurt Bush's chances of reelection, costing him support in several key states."

28.   Budapest Agreement & the US Taxpayers Money

A lot has been said in the past 4 years about the Budapest Agreement.

That is why there will be only two new aspects briefly mentioned in this aspect - material and reputational.

MATERIAL

During one of his foreign trips to Europe in 2017, a top US official of the newly elected President Trump administration allegedly asked a question in public: "Why should the US taxpayers care about Ukraine?" That question actually did a lot of good to Ukraine, because the multiple answers to that question did clarify the matter. The public answer seems to have changed the opinion of that top official as well.

If summarized. The following can be said:

Ukraine actually saved US taxpayers a lot of money.

How is that?

A former Ukraine's Minister of Defence during his speech at a central Ukrainian channel stated that by his information, the United States had to spend at least $ 10 billion annually on countermeasures against the rockets stationed on Ukraine's territory alone.

24 years X $ 10 bln = Quarter of the Trillion roughly without inflation, etc.

If the number appears steep, here are some basic facts of what Ukraine had at the time:

It possessed 1,900 strategic nuclear warheads and had between 2,650 and 4,200 tactical nuclear weapons deployed on its territory.

There were 176 ICBMs located in Ukraine: 130 SS-19 ICBMs each with 6 nuclear warheads, and 46 SS-24 ICBMs each with 10 nuclear warheads. Additional 14 SS-24 missiles were present, but were not deployed with warheads.

In addition there were 44 strategic bombers armed with some 600 air-launched missiles and gravity bombs as well.

2. Ukraine spared the US taxpayers future expenses.

If Russia had occupied just Eastern Ukraine, it would have increased its military-industrial potential almost in half - Ukrainian missile plants would have resumed the production of the most dangerous rockets, probably SS-18 including; the nuclear warheads would have most likely returned on Ukraine's territory just like they may have already returned to Crimea.

There is also a tank plant in Kharkiv in Northern Ukraine which produces tanks exceeding Russian ones on all parameters, according to many specialists. It is the same plant that started production of the most famous tank of WW II - the T-34 by the way.

So, for Putin, Ukraine may have well become what Chechoslovakia had become for Hitler after the Munich Agreement and before the WW II- another industrial heart working toward the war. The situation with Munich Agreement shows that there is not appeasing the aggressor.

It's just by trying to do so, the civilized world accrues future inevitable expenses at the terribly high interest rate.

REPUTATIONAL

Of course, it's better for the Westerners not to know what Ukrainians thought of their Western leaders after they discovered themselves empty-handed against one of the most ruthless armies in the world.

The most popular ironic GIF on Ukrainian internet of those days was the scene from "The Fifth Element" movie where during the shootout with the Mangalores on the spaceship Bruce Willis asks a guy in the wig to throw him a gun. And receives billiard balls instead. On the picture, Bruce Willis is marked with the Ukrainian flag, of course, the guy in the wig - as the collective West.

Well, there were some politicians in the West who dared call the situation the proper name.

In her interview to Handelsblatt in 2017, Germany's Defense Minister Ursula von der Leyen warned American President Trump on suggested "Nuclear Deal" with Putin, saying "Ukraine has already been duped once on this question."

There were American politicians who warned that such treatment of Ukraine would have a domino effect on all the system of the world guarantees.

Below are the words of the former US ambassador to Ukraine Steven Pifer in his 2014 article for the Brookings Institute:

"If a North Korean diplomat were to ask his or her Ukrainian counterpart how the Budapest memorandum worked out, the response would not be a happy one. At a September conference in Kyiv, former President Leonid Kuchma, who signed the Budapest memorandum for Ukraine, said that Ukraine had been "cheated." Prime Minister Arseniy Yatseniuk referred to the "notorious" Budapest memorandum. Such comments do not make good advertisements for future security assurances.

157

Washington cannot undo Russia's violations. It can and should, however, do more to fulfill its obligations under the Budapest memorandum by doing more to bolster Ukraine and penalize Russia until Moscow alters its policy. Such U.S. action could also change the Ukrainian narrative in the hypothetical conversation with a North Korean diplomat to "the Russians violated the memorandum, but the Americans backed us to the fullest and made Moscow pay." That would help restore credibility to security assurances as an element in the toolkit of America's non-proliferation diplomacy."

Luckily, the beginning of the year 2018 shows that Washington finally heeded what people like Mr. Pifer and Sen. John McCain have been saying about supporting Ukraine past several years.

29. Carol of the Bells, Summertime, Cassie Cisyk

The Ukrainian folk songs are so melodic, that many people do not even imagine how they influenced the world modern classic.

The Ukrainian language is considered to be one of the most melodic in the world. For example, according to 1934 Paris linguistic contest, it was recognized as #3 after French and Persian. Current musicians tend to rank it #2 after Italian though.

Anyway, it's up to you to make your own opinion based on a couple of following examples:

CAROL OF THE BELLS

Although "Carol of the Bells" has become a popular tune during the winter holidays, the original version of the song had nothing to do with Christmas.

Actually, it was a Ukrainian folk "winter well-wishing song" with the melody resembling a swallow's trill or twitter. It was one of many songs sung in Ukrainian villages.

Ukrainian composer Mykola Leontovych recorded the first version of this melody in 1901, but only on December 25, 1916, the student choir of St. Volodymyr University – currently Taras Shevchenko University in Kiev – conducted by Alexander Koshetz performed it for the first time.

The lyrics of "Shedryk" are the following:

A little swallow flew in
and started to twitter,
to summon the master:
"Come out, come out, O master,,
look at the sheep pen,
there the ewes have yeaned
and the lambkins have been born
Your goods and livestock are great,
you will have a lot of money.
If not money, then chaff
you have a dark-eyebrowed beautiful wife."
Shchedryk, shchedryk, a shchedrivka,
A little swallow flew in

It should be noted that 'Shchedryk' was composed and performed during a difficult time in Ukraine in the period after the WW 1 and on the eve of Revolution described in one of the previous chapters of this book titled "Two Independent Ukraines".

In 1919 choir conductor and composer Aleksander Kozhets was mandated by a Ukrainian government to create the Ukrainian National Chorus and promote Ukrainian music in major cultural centers in the West. Touring across Europe and North and South America, the chorus performed over 1,000 concerts.

The Ukrainian National Chorus introduced its program including Shedryk to the United States to a sold-out audience in Carnegie Hall Oct. 5, 1921.

When American choir director Peter Wilhousky heard Leontovych's work, it reminded him of bells. He copyrighted the new lyrics in 1936 and also published the song, despite the fact that the work had been published in Ukraine many before him.

That is the story how already "Carol of the Bells" became associated with Christmas.

As for Mykola Leontovych, one of the most talented Ukrainian composers, he was shot by a Bolshevik agent one winter day in January 1921.

SUMMERTIME

Some consider it classic, others - one of the best pop songs of all times.

Probably every American has heard this melody at least couple of times in his lifetime.

"Summertime" has been recorded over 33,000 times by the musicians of different nationalities and in absolutely different styles. Versions of this song made the pop charts numerous times.

It may be a surprise to some, but many musicians including Ukrainian-Canadian composer and singer Alexis Cochan believe that this world-famous song was created after George Gershvin heard a Ukrainian lullaby "Oi, Khodyt Son Kolo Vikon" ("A Dream Passes By The Windows") at a New York City performance by the aforementioned Ukrainian National Chorus in 1929 at the same Carnegie Hall. By the way, Gershwin's father was a Ukrainian immigrant.

So, every time one hears the "Summertime" performed even by singers such as Abbie Mitchell, Leontyne Price, Ella Fitzgerald & Louis Armstrong, Miles Davis, Janis Joplin, Billie Holiday, Willie Nelson, Scarlett Johansson, Sublime, and Harolyn Blackwell, - one can easily imagine listening to the melody of the lullaby created and first sung in Ukraine.

It's easy to find that song on the web and try to imagine a Ukrainian mother singing the following words to her child centuries before the tune became popular worldwide:

The Dream passes by the window,
And Sleep (walks) by the fence.
The Dream asks the Sleep:
- Where shall we spend the night?

Where the cottage is warm,
Where the baby is tiny,
There we will go,
And rock the child to sleep.

There we will sleep
And rock the child
Sleep, sleep, my dear,
Sleep, sleep, my little dove.

CASSIE CISYK

This original lullaby is best performed in Ukrainian by the renown Kvitka Cisyk, better known to the American audience as Cassie.

"Kvitka" was her true name which in Ukrainian means "Flower" and the name Cassie is derived from the abbreviation of her first and last name - K.C.

She was born on April 4, 1953, in New York's Queens, in the family of Ivanna and Volodymir Cisyk, post-war immigrants from western Ukraine.

Volodymir Cisyk, a well-known Ukrainian concert violinist and teacher, taught his daughter the violin since she was 5 training her for a career of a classical musician.

Kvitka Cisyk had a very rare coloratura soprano timbre and her voice was known by probably almost every American largely due to her singing in musical jingles used in TV and radio commercials for such companies as Ford, Coca-Cola, American Airlines, McDonald's.

She sang the "Have you driven a Ford lately?" and "You deserve a break today!" jingles which became hits in themselves.

Apart from jingles, Kvitka also pursued a career in three other different musical genres: popular music, classical opera, and Ukrainian folk music.

Cisyk recorded the original version of "You Light Up My Life", the song that would bring the Best Song Oscar in 1977 to a different singer.

In 1990, Kvitka Cisyk's collection of Ukrainian folk songs was nominated for Grammy in the category Best album of contemporary folk music.

After Ukraine gained its independence, Kvitka wanted to give a series of concerts in the country. Unfortunately, her concert plans did not come true because of her illness.

The names of the two albums of Ukrainian folk songs Kvitka Cisyk recorded on her own money are:

"Songs of Ukraine" & "My Two Colors"

(For those who would like to listen to Cassie singing in Ukrainian).

30. The Fifth Element, Lagertha, Curly the Cowboy

THE FIFTH ELEMENT

Mila "The Fifth Element" Jovovich - born in Kiev and often calls herself "a humble Ukrainian girl".

Mila's words on her Facebook January 30, 2014, during Ukrainian Revolution of Dignity, meant a lot to many people in Ukraine:

"I sit watching the news and my heart hurts so badly when I see my incredible, Ukrainian brothers and sisters suffering for what they believe. I pray so much that a peaceful solution will be found. Ukraine, I BELIEVE IN YOU!"

Mila's mother too was an actress at the Ukrainian Cinema Studio named after Dovzhenko.

(Oleksandr Dovzhenko's silent "Earth" filmed in 1930 was recognized by UNESCO among 5 World Masterpieces).

Mila Jovovich nicely sings Ukrainian folk songs and there is even a studio version of her singing "Solovei Schebeche" (Nightingale Chirps) available on Youtube.

LAGERTHA

Katherine "Lagertha" Winnick - born Katerina Anna Vinitska in the family of Ukrainian emigrants, spoke only Ukrainian until she was 8 years old. Loves and supports Ukraine, treasures her Ukrainian ancestry and asks the world not to forget what trials Ukraine had to withstand in its recent history.

There is her brief comment available on Youtube before American premiere of "Bitter Harvest" movie about Holodomor where she call on the audience to be aware of it.

With all the martial arts achievements, Katherine looks quite natural in the ranks of great Ukrainian women-warriors mentioned earlier in this book

Besides, her getting to play one of the most memorable Viking characters in the popular TV series, may not be that coincidental considering Viking influence in the country of her origin, Ukraine-Kiev Rus.

Katherine's mother is a Vice-President of the Ukrainian Canadian Congress.

CURLEY, THE COWBOY

At the age of 73, Jack Palance won the Best Supporting Actor Oscar for his work in "City Slickers" and went on to perform one-armed pushups on the stage during his acceptance speech, which official Academy Award site names as one of the most unforgettable moments in the history of Oscar.

Jack Palance was born Volodymyr Palahniuk.

Jack's daughter Holly, during her recent visit to Ukraine, said the following:

"To go from a coal miner to a movie star is a big deal. My father had the work ethic that I've witnessed here (in Ukraine). I was so impressed."

"When I was a little girl I was aware that my father had Ukrainian ancestry because we, although we lived in Los Angeles, we would go to Pennsylvania to visit my grandparents. And my grandmother was a fantastic cook."

Ms. Holly Palance who herself played in movies like "The Omen" and "The Best of Times," also mentions the situation that happened some time ago and which Canadian press describes this way:

"Perhaps Jack's most Ukrainian moment came in 2004 when he was invited to the awards ceremony for the "Russian Nights" Art festival, to win the "Russian People's Choice Award" along with Dustin Hoffman. In accepting his award, Dustin Hoffman noted that his grandparents came from "Kiev, Russia" and expressed gratitude to the "Russian people". After being introduced, Palance said: "I feel like I walked into the wrong room by mistake. I think that Russian film is interesting, but I have nothing to do with Russia or Russian film. My parents were born in Ukraine: I'm Ukrainian. I am not Russian. So, excuse me, but I do not belong here. It's best if we leave".

Jack Palance, screen actor of Ukrainian descent, dressed in Ukrainian national attire, holding the ancient Ukrainian instrument Bandura. He will participate in the Concert during the Ukrainian celebrations in Toronto, Ont., Canada on October 11, 1964.

For those who would like to hear Jack's voice again and at the same time learn what Ukraine had to go through in the previous century, there is a Canadian documentary *Between Hitler & Stalin: Ukraine in WWII. Untold Story* narrated by the great Ukrainian Cowboy.

Point of Interest. In case you did not know, NATALIE WOOD's real name was Natalia Zakharenko. Her grandparents had to leave the city of Kharkiv, Ukraine, because of "Russian Revolution". Although born in the US, Natalie spoke Russian with Ukrainian accent. According to "Natasha: The Biography of Natalie Wood" by Suzanne Finstad, for one of her Hollywood roles she had to "fine-tune her Russian dialect.. to lose her parents' Ukrainian accent."

EPILOGUE

Just recently on its own initiative, Russia conducted quite representative "nation DNA test." It showed that predominantly its population belongs to the Finn-Ugric group with a considerable portion of Tatars. The true "close-kin" nations to Russia are Finland and Hungary.

Not Ukraine.

It has been obvious all the time that the nations with such different national clothes, traditions, dances, cuisines cannot be one and the same people.

Ukrainian Hopak dance, which actually was a demonstration of military skills has nothing in common with Russian Kalinka.

And even 30 Russian 3-stringed balalaikas cannot replace one Ukrainian bandura which has up to 68 strings. This two national music instruments can tell a lot about two nations' differences if one comes to think about it.

The test ruins two myths at once.

Like DNA paternity test, it proves that Russia is not a "brother", not even a "cousin" or relative to Ukraine. Although it did behave like the Biblical Cain toward Abel for the past several centuries.

Nor it is a heir to Kiev Rus' legacy which was the confederation of Slavic tribes with Vikings at its core.

In that sense, current Croatians have much more rights to claim that they are "brotherly nation" to Ukrainians for example, but not Russians.

In all aspects, current Russia has the same legacy rights to Kiev Rus history, as, for example, the current country of Romania would have on the legacy of Roman Empire.

One day Russia may even have to return the name "Russia" to Ukraine by the way - Ukrainian Parliament is working towards it, and current precedent of one country having to change its name as in case with Macedonia and Greece shows that it is well possible.

Ukraine will surely do everything to return its stolen identity and achievements Muscovy appropriated. There are also tens thousands of ancient books, paintings, and artefacts Moscow and Saint Petersburg will have to return to Kiev.

While on topic of genetics, it is hard not to mention that according to the Cambridge Professor Dr. Peter Forster, a geneticist specializing in the research of the prehistoric origins and ancestry of mankind, there were only two places in Europe during the Ice Age where people could live continuously – it is the territory of the current Spain and southern France, and the territory of Ukraine. It is from these two territories, in his opinion, the whole Europe was populated.

The oldest house in the world is the 15,000 years old one made of mammoth bones was found near Kiev, Ukraine:

A recently discovered not far from Kiev Trypillya Culture which turns out to be more ancient than even the Egyptian one, can have the clue to many questions.

In other words, people, we now call Vikings, may first have migrated to Scandinavia from the current day Ukraine and simply returned to their historic Motherland and their own several centuries later.

So, as funny as it may sound now, many nations of Europe, such as the Swedes in particular, may turn out to be "Ukrainians." The similar colors of Ukrainian and Swedish flags are not accidental in any way.

Actually, Dr. Forster already has some initial results on this matter, - couple of years ago he took part in the "DNA-portrait of the nation" run be a central Ukrainian TV channel. There were couple of moments in the program when he looked quite surprised. I guess Dr. Forster needed more time to check and double check the results before making the official statement. The program is on Youtube by the way, and although it is in Ukrainian, it is quite clear what Dr. Forster says in English.

Territory of Ukraine was also a place of the Scythian Kingdom and one of the most famous pieces of Scythian gold was found in Ukraine too. It is beautifully-detailed, fourth century B.C. Pectoral (necklace) with three rows of incredibly detailed images. These include warriors making a sheepskin garment, winged griffins tackling a horse, a mare nursing its foal, a young shepherd milking an ewe, lions ripping apart pigs, deer, sheep, dogs and grasshoppers.

It is on display in Kiev-Pechersk Lavra.

Below is the monument to the legendary founders of the city of Kiev – three brothers Kyi, Schek, Horyv and their sister Lybid. According to some historians, the city was founded in 482 AD, centuries before the first Vikings were first mentioned. But does not the whole appearance of the composition including the boat resemble the one of the Vikings? Sister Lybid surely looks like Lagertha to me.

Now we can return to present times and the title of this book.

"The United States and the State of Minnesota have benefited tremendously from the innovative spirit, rich culture and heritage, and determined work ethic of our Ukrainian-American residents; and now, therefore I, Governor of Minnesota, do hereby proclaim Wednesday, August 24, 2016 Ukrainian Independence Day."

Of course, there are much more instances of Ukraine's influencing the lives of the Americans than the described in this book.

There are companies like PetCube, Grammarly, Looksery, LiquidPiston that provide unique solutions to previously existed problems.

There is also Kievan Alexander Kokush, recipient of two Technical Oscars for his invention of extendible camera-holding arm which made the filming of Titanic movie most memorable scenes under the angles never imagined before.

Some American beekeeping associations celebrate the birth anniversary of Petro Prokopovych, the Father of Commercial Beekeeping because of his inventing of beehive frames and other inventions.

Not many Americans know that the only other language apart from English spoken at the home of a little Wayne Gretzky was Ukrainian. There is a Youtube video of 2014 titled "United for Ukraine" where Mr. Gretzky talks about it in his public address in greater details.

Hope that soon more American States will be celebrating Ukrainian Independence Day!

Conclusion, Contacts

Dear Reader,

Hope you discovered something new and interesting for yourself in this book! I hope that many links and references in it will be useful in discovering more about Ukraine!

It's my first experience at writing a book, so, surely there are things I could have done better and sentences I could have composed in a more flowing style.

Please do not be too hard on me for that – actually, you can help me improve the book!

Since it is an electronic book, I can make correction to the book, basically, online.

So, please send me your comments and suggestions to my email

a.lazko@yahoo.com

You are more than welcome to visit my personal site

www.U-Krane.com

(it is more like a trial version yet, and a new one is coming soon)

I will use the slogan of the site here:

"FEEL LIKE CRANE – WELLFLY TO UKRAINE"

P.S. In the summer of 2017 Mr. Steven Wozniak came to Kiev with his wife. After the trip he said that one of his 4 life-long dreams had come true. Yes, Mr. Wozniak has a "Crane" in him (considers himself partly Ukrainian).

Steve Wozniak's IBM partner, Mr. Lubomyr Romankiw, the inventor of Thin Film Magnetic Heads, who was inducted in the National Inventors Hall of Fame in Washington together with Steve Jobs, is seen in the streets of his native Lviv from time to time.

These are Dr. Romankiw's words in one of his interviews: "When you start your PC, seven of my patents are at play. When you first push the key and an image flashes on the screen, it is also my invention – magnetic heads that make a recording on the disk. The heads I designed are thinner than a human hair. When you type letters, it is also my work."

Monument to King Vladimir the Great, Kiev.
It is above the place on the Dnieper River, where most likely Kiev Rus was
baptized into Christianity.

Moxel, Golden Horde, Muscovy

Starting 1854, Count Aleksey Sergeyevich Uvarov, a Russian archeologist often considered to be the founder of the study of the prehistory of Russia and the President of the Moscow Archaeological Society, excavated 7,729 mounds in the area of central Russia and summarized his findings in *The Meryans and Their Lifestyle as Shown by Kurgan Excavations.*

Here is what *Wikipedia* tells now: "The Merya people inhabited a territory corresponding roughly to what is now the area of the Golden Ring of Russia or Zalesye region of Russia, including the modern-day Moscow, Yaroslavl, Kostroma, Ivanovo, and Vladimir oblasts. The five Volga Finnic groups are the Merya, Mari, Muromians, Meshchera and Mordvins."

The very core of present-day Russia, the "Golden Ring" was and is the homeland of the Volga Finnic groups.

That in itself is a huge blow to all those who say that Ukrainians and Russians are one people or one nation.

Having unearthed almost eight thousand burial mounds, Count Uvarov did not find a single (!) Slavic burial mound among them. Uvarov could not find even a single Kiev coin! It means that Meryan land did not have any significant economic relation with Kiev Rus.

And that is another blow – there was no noticeable interaction between the two realms.

The Meryan people lived in forests in small huts, speaking their language, worshiping their gods, and had their own culture.

The fact that out of 300 coins of the 9-12th centuries found by Uvarov, 180 were of Asian origin means their trade ties were mostly eastbound.

The first interaction between Kiev Rus and the Meryan people started only in the 12th century, when

Yuri Dolgorukiy, one of the youngest of Kiev princes, came to that land in 1137. According to a Russian myth, he was the one who founded the city of Moscow in 1147, but that is just not true. And here is one of the reasons why - Yuri's son Vsevolod the Big Nest, who ruled in that land afterward, dividing the cities between his many sons, did not mention any Moscow.

He did not mention Novgorod too by the way. And it looks like the Meryan land did not have much interaction with that city also.

The Greek route

Novgorod was not just a city. It was a Republic with close ties to Kiev. Vladimir the Great of Kiev baptized Novgorod's inhabitants in 989, the year after he had baptized Kiev. In 1019 Yaroslav the Wise of Kiev granted Novgorod a charter of self-government, - the town assembly, or *veche*, received the right to elect their ruler.

According to the Harvard Professor Richard Pipes, Novgorod and Kiev were the two terminal points of the "Rout from the Varangians to the Greeks". The Normans had their names for those two cities where *Holmgard* was the name for Novgorod and Kiev was called *Konugard*. Kiev was the largest city of the rout and became the headquarters of it. As a result, the predominantly Slavic tribes living along that trade route formed along the Dnieper river, communicated easily with each other and belonged to one civilizational realm.

The Meryan culture was formed along the Volga river and the civilizational gap between the two cultures was immense. The Lipitsa Battle fought at the Lipitsa River on April 21–22, 1216, can be used as an example of that gap.

One side in the battle was the Novgorodians, supported by their allies - the princes of Pskov and Smolensk (all three are the Slavic cities), on another side – all the might of the Meryan land under the command of the two of Vsevolod's sons. One of the Vsevolod's sons, Yaroslav, the future father of Aleksandr "Nevsky", boasted that the Meryans under his command exceeded the Novgorodians in a proportion of "hundred to one".

It was the first major battle between the Slavic tribes against the Finnish ones. The outcome was startling – the Meryans lost 9,233 killed, the Novgorodians – 5 (five) people in all. The incredible proportion of 1 to almost 2,000 in losses shows that one side did not know who its opponent was, and how technologically superior it was as well.

22 years after this battle, the Mongol invasion took place. It was the year 1238.

French King's ambassador to the Golden Horde

In the year 1254, a Pope and a French King sent their emissary to Batu Khan, who had his camp at the Volga river. The emissary was Friar William Rubruck, one of the most educated people of that time. He had a letter from the French King to Batu's son Sartak, who was believed to have become a Christian. The goal was to get permission to spread Catholicism among Sartak people.

Friar Rubruck started his journey from Constantinople where he stayed after the Crusade of 1249 with King Louis. Here is what the editors of The Journey to the Eastern Parts of the World describe in the foreword:

"I would only venture to add to this well-deserved praise of Friar William, bestowed on him by the greatest authority on medieval geography of our century that not only was he keen and intelligent, but conscientious and thorough in a high degree. The study of his narrative shows his careful preparation for his work as an explorer... he had read historical works and the classical poets, and had specially noted

178

the movements Europewards of the tribes of western Asia since the time of the great Hunnic invasions: which latter presented to his mind many striking analogies with the Mongol ones just over. While preparing for his journey at Constantinople in the winter and spring of 1253.

Let us now note what Friar William was able to add by his journey and careful observations to Europe's sum of general and geographical knowledge. His principal contributions to geographical science were the indication of the true sources and course of the Don and Volga, the lake nature of the Caspian. To him linguistics and anthropology owe the first accurate information on the Goths of the Crimean coast, on the identity of the Comans with the Kipchak, Turks and Cangle, on the difference between the Tartars and the Mongols, on the connexity of the languages of the Bashkirds (Pascatir) and the Hungarians, on the origin of the Danubian Bulgarians, on the affinity between the languages of the Russians, Poles, Bohemians and Slavs and that of the Wandals. He was the first to describe the Christian communities in the Mongol empire, and to give details of their rituals and the tenets of their faith. ...King Louis must have complied with Friar William's request, for we learn from Roger Bacon that he met the traveler in France a few years later, and conversed with him about his discoveries and adventures. We know that he made a careful examination of his report, nearly every geographical detail of which we find embodied in his famous Opus Majus."

That is how thorough William Rubruck's work was.

Moxel

According to the editors of his book, Rubruck was "the first, since Herodotus, to locate correctly the sources of the Don, which flows out of Ivan Lake in Tula," so when the Friar was personally reading the following passage to the French King in the year 1255, he knew exactly what area and population he was describing:

"The country beyond the Tanais (Don) is most beautiful, with rivers and forests. To the north are great forests, inhabited by two races of men: to wit, **the Moxel**, who are without any religion, a race of pure pagans. They have no towns, but only little hamlets in the forest. Their chief and the greater part of them were killed in Germany; for the Tartars took them with them to the borders of Germany, and so they have formed a high opinion of the Germans, and they hope that through them they may finally be freed of the Tartar yoke. If a trader comes among this people, he with whom he first puts up must provide for him as long as he sees fit to stay among them. If one sleeps with another's wife the husband cares not unless he sees it with his own eyes; so they are not jealous. They have swine, honey and wax, precious furs and hawks."

There is no doubt that the Friar describes the same Meryan land described at the beginning of this chapter, - in the footnotes the editors of the book make the comment: "The Moxel and Merdas form the two branches of the Finnish Mordvin people. These names, according to Pallas (Voyages), correctly transcribed are Mokshad and Ersad, the first name being applied by them to their race in general. The earliest mention I have found of this people is in Jornandes, where he speaks of the Mordensimnis among the peoples of Hermanaric's empire. Constantine Porphyrogenitus refers also to the Mordia country. Nestor (Chronique) calls them Mordwa. Pian de Carpine speaks of them as Morduani."

So many amazing things just one quote reveals! Firstly, the people in Moxel country are still pagans in 1254! As a reminder, Kiev Rus was baptized into Christianity in 988 and Novgorod a year later. A very painful blow to Moscow church's claims of a spiritual legacy!

Secondly, William Rubruck says in his report that it was a separate country in itself and had the name of Moxel. Another famous historian Constantine Porphyrogenitus says it was a country too.

Thirdly, it did not have "any towns, but only little hamlets in the forests" in 1255! Their cities such as Suzdal, Rostov or Vladimir

Zalesky were in fact "the fenced villages" according to a Russian historian S.M. Soloviov.

Fourthly, the Meryans participated on the side of the Tatars in the invasion of Germany. Yuri, one of Vsevolod The Big Nest sons was the chief who, according to Rubruck, was killed "with the greater part of them" trying to conquer Germans in the year 1241.

The Mongols left Yury's brother Yaroslav, the one who had lost in the Lipitza battle described above, to rule in the Rostov-Suzdal, Moxel land. But, as was the rule in the Golden Horde, Yaroslav had to give his eight-year-old son Alexander as a hostage (amanat) to the Khan. Alexander spent 14 years among the Mongols and learned the structure, language, and customs of the Golden Horde. Batu khan liked Alexander so much that allowed him to become a blood brother to his son Sartak (the one whom William Rubruck will be sent to visit several years later). There is also information that Alexander married the daughter of Batu Khan.

Alexander, who will later be named by the Russian historians as "Nevsky," being a hostage and being too young, could not have possibly taken part in the Nevsky battle for which he was ascribed his name. Besides, as it turns out, that was not a battle, but a skirmish involving up to 300 people on both sides.

There was another reason to name him "Nevsky" though – during the population census of 1257 conducted by the Mongols, Alexander together with the Mongols subdues Novgorod.

Moscow

Interesting fact, but even during that population census of 1257, there was no Moscow mentioned, and the Mongols were scrupulous enough to mention even little villages, is it not strange?

Let us read another quote from a Harvard Professor Richard Pipes' book *Russia Under the Old Regime*:

"In the policy of collaboration (with the Mongols), no one excelled the branch of Nevsky's family ensconced in what in the thirteenth century was the insignificant **Moscow** appanage carved out in **1276** for Nevsky's son, Danil Aleksandrovich. Danil's son, Iurii, managed in 1317 to secure for himself the hand of the khan's sister and the title to Vladimir to go with it."

Here it is. Here is Moscow! Only in 1276, and carved out by the Mongols as a present to the family who collaborated the most!

One can understand easily now why later on Moscow created the myth of its foundation by a Kiev prince and almost 130 years earlier the actual date, can one not? But the truth is - Moscow was established and granted a legal basis through the yarlyk (patent) of Khan Menghu Timur only in 1272. Prince Yury Dolgorukiy has nothing to do with Moscow whatsoever.

By the way, Yury was expelled from the Meryan land by his first son – Andrey Bogolyubskiy. He had to return to Kiev where, historians agree, he was poisoned. Just recently his remains were found near one of the Kiev-Pechersk cathedrals. According to anthropologists, his arms were truly a bit longer than usual.

Let us quickly see how Moscow became the center of that land, what forces eventually made it the capital.

Richard Pipes again: "Moscow (without Vladimir and the Grand Princely title, however) passed to his younger brother, Ivan Danilovich, later designated Ivan 1 of Russia. The new ruler proved an extraordinarily gifted and unscrupulous political manipulator. By one scholar's estimate, he spent most of his reign either at Sarai (Golden Horde's capital on the Volga) or en route to or from it, which gives some idea how busy he must have been intriguing there

In 1327, the population of Tver rose against the Mongols and massacred a high-level deputation sent from Sarai to oversee the collection of the tribute. After some hesitation, the prince of Tver sided with the rebels. As soon as this news had reached him, Ivan left for

182

Sarai. He returned as the head of a combined Mongol-Russian punitive force which so devastated Tver and a great deal of central Russia besides that the region was not yet fully recovered half a century later. As a reward for his loyalty, the Mongols invested Ivan with the title of Great Prince and appointed him Farmer General of the tribute throughout Russia.

This was undoubtedly an expensive privilege since it made Ivan responsible for the arrears and defaults of others, but one that offered him unique opportunities for meddling in the internal affairs of rival appanages. Control of the tribute meant in effect monopoly of access to the khan's court. Taking advantage of it, Ivan and his successors forbade the other princes to enter into direct relations with any other state, the Horde included, except through the agency of Moscow. In this manner, Moscow gradually isolated its rivals and moved to the forefront as the intermediary between the conqueror and his Russian subjects. The Mongols had no cause to regret the favors they had heaped on Ivan. In the twelve remaining years of his life, he served them no less ably than his grandfather Alexander Nevsky had done, keeping in line, with force when necessary, Novgorod, Rostov, Smolensk and any other city that dared to raise its head. Karl Marx, whom the communist government of Russia regarded as an authoritative historian, characterized this first prominent representative of the Moscow line as a blend of 'the characters of the Tartar's hangman, sycophant and slave-in-chief.'"

Given the facts mentioned above, whose legacy can Moscow claim? Any room to claim the legacy of the great democratic Novgorod? Aleksander Nevsky ruined its independence and brought it to slavery. Ivan I stabbed it several times and let it bleed, just like Ivan III. Ivan IV basically killed it and what was left afterward was just a carcass of the great city.

To any unbiased reader, it is obvious whose "genes" run in Moscovy even in our days. In Richard Pipes' opinion, Muscovy differed from every other State in Europe in that it had no concept of private property because everything had been regarded as the property of the Farmer of the tribute. "The Mongol influence ensured that Russia would be an autocratic state with values fundamentally different from those of Western civilization."

Karl Marx was even more categorical in diagnosing that formation:

"The bloody mire of Mongolian slavery, not the rude glory of the Norman epoch, forms the cradle of Muscovy, and modern Russia is but a metamorphosis of Muscovy."

Point to stress

Even if we suppose that the Meryan land had become a part of the Kiev Rus realm during the roughly 100 years period before the Mongol invasion, would it be reasonable to assume that this distant and culturally different province had any right to claim the legacy of Kiev Rus?

It would be hard to imagine Britain claiming the legacy of Normandy or France on the reason that William the Conqueror came from that area, would it not?

Here is what Dr. Edward Clark, whose *Travels in Russia* we quoted earlier in the book, wrote in 1800:

"Until his time (of Peter I), however, Tartars were lords of Moscow with the tsars themselves being obliged to stand in the presence of their ambassadors, while the latter sat at meat, and to endure the most humiliating ceremonies. Basilovich shook off the Tartar yoke; but it was a long time before the Russians, always children of imitation, ceased to mimic a people by whom they had been conquered. They had neither arts nor opinions of their own: everything in Moscow was Tartarian - dress, manners, buildings, equipages, in short, all except religion and language."

Kievan Rus' - Kyivan Rus' (1220-1240)
The Kyivan Rus' federation after 12th century continued to disintegrate and Kyiv itself lost its primacy: the city was sacked several times by feuding princes, most notably in 1169 by Andrei Bogoliubskii. The quarreling between the princes left Rus' incl. later Ukrainian territory vulnerable to foreign attacks, and the invasion of the Mongols or the Golden Horde in 1236–40 finally destroyed the state.
Historical maps of Ukraine
Kingdom of Sweden
Uppsala
Danish Estonia
Order of the Livonian Brothers
Novgorod Republic
Novgorod
Pskov
Grand Principality of Vladimir-Suzdal
1238
Vladimir
since 1169
Volga
Bilyar
Bolgar
1236
Bulgars
Murom-Ryazan
Ryazan
1237
Kingdom of Denmark
Baltic sea
Zemai-čiai
Lithu-anians
Trakai
Polotsk
Smolensk
1238
Kozelsk
Vschyzh
Golden Horde
Teutonic Order
Pru-sai
Gdansk
Pomo-rania
Grodno
Starodub
Novhorod-Siverskyi
Kursk
Gniezno
Masovia
Kiechesk
Pinsk
Liubech
Chernihiv
Greater Poland
Kuyavia
Berestya
Turov
Metropolitan seat
Pulyvl
Holy
Kingdom of Poland
Vyshgorod
Pryluk
Romen
Donec
Sarai
Halych-
Holm
Luck
Kyiv (Kiev)
Pereyaslavl
Silesia
Lesser Poland
Kraków
Volodymyr
Yuriyiv
Kaniv
Kingdom of
Roman
Bohemia
Peremyshl
Kolodiazhyn
Korsun
Halych
Terebovl
Kalius
since 1199
1240/1245
Vasyliv
Esztergom
Empire
Kingdom of Hungary
Bilgorod
Chersonesos
Black sea
Hungarian
Kingdom of Croatia
Empire of Trnovo
Adriatic sea
Kingdom of Rashka (Serbia)
Bulgaria
Empire of Trebizond
km
500
1000
Constantinople
1204–1261
Latin Empire
1204
1204–1261
Empire of Nicaea
Nicaea
Seljuks

Correction. According to William Rubruck and other facts mentioned in this chapter, the Vladimir-Suzdal and Murom-Ryazan principalities should be in different color and titled as Moxel, a different country and not part of Rus.

Kingdom of Galich, Lithuania, Heirs of Rus

Friar John de Carpine

Some 5 years prior his future trip to the Mongols, and, probably not even aware of it looming, Friar William Rubruck, mentioned in the previous chapter, was at the King Louis' court listening, together with the King, to the reports of two other friars who had just returned from the trip to the Golden Horde.

The two travelers reporting to the King were Friar John of Pian de Carpine and his companion, Friar Benedict of Poland who had delivered a letter from the Pope to Kuyuk Khan in northern Mongolia. They returned to Lyon in 1248 and the Pope sent them to the King seeking to delay King's setting out for the Holy Land.

The report did not delay the King's departure but was used by William Rubruck in his preparations for his mission later on.

So, when one reads *Journey of Friar John of Pian de Carpine to the Court of Kuyuk Khan, 1245-1247*, one may imagine the French King listening and William of Rubruck reading it back in the middle of the 13th century.

The story unfolds with Friars Carpine and Benedict starting their trip to the East from Lyons on April 16, 1245.

When they were still in Poland, Friar John de Carpine reports: "At that time, through God's special grace, the Lord Vassilko, Duke of Ruscia, had come there, from whom we learned more accurately of the Tartars: for he had sent his ambassadors to them, who had come back to him and to his brother Daniel, bearing to the lord Daniel a safe conduct to go to Batu."

Friar de Carpine uses a Latin transcription of the name Rus/Ruthenia – "Ruscia", and the two princes he meets are very important figures in the history of Kiev Rus. We will meet them later in the friar's story.

"Thence then, by the grace of God... we came to Kiew, which is the metropolis of Ruscia" - thanks to this first-hand witness, we know for sure that although Kiev was seriously damaged and lost most of its population, it remained the spiritual center of Rus even five years after the Mongol invasion.

There was a Khan's representative in Kiev it seems since John de Carpine mentions a Millenarius who helped them with the horses, but the first city he specifically mentions as being under the direct Mongol rule was the city of Kanev some 100 km south of Kiev on the other side of the Dnieper river.

Another interesting fact Pian de Carpine state is that "beyond Ruscia to the north is Pruscia, which has all been recently conquered by the Teutonic knights." At first, it is hard to imagine how it is possible, but when you add present-day Belarus and Lithuania to Kiev Rus realm, you will see it the way the traveler viewed the political map. We will talk about it later too, but it is interesting to note that Friar William Rubruck from the previous chapter names the Don river as "the eastern boundary of Ruscia."

On reaching that river, John de Carpine in his turn makes a very similar geographic comment about different countries in that area Friar Rubruck will make several years later: "Comania hath to the north of it, immediately after Ruscia, the Morduins, the Bilers, or great Bulgaria."

As one can see, Friar John also distinguishes Mordwins, which is another name for the Meryans, as a separate country. Not even part of Rus.

In his report, Friar John mentions meeting at Batu's camp the son of the prince Yaroslav, future Alexander "Nevsky". And it looks like in some instances, Alexander was even translating to the khan for him.

On completing their mission, the two friars returned the same way: "We reached (Kiew) fifteen days before the feast of Saint John the Baptist (9th June). The Kiewans who had heard of our arrival all came out to meet us rejoicing, and congratulated us as if we had risen from the dead, and so they did to us throughout Ruscia, Poland and Bohemia."

John de Carpine notes that he met at Kiev several Constantinople traders and that all of them were Italians. He even mentions among others Michel of Genoa, Manuel of Venice, and Nicolas of Pisa. It is another invaluable witness of Kiev being an international trade center just 5 years after the Mongol invasion.

The two friars also reported that Danylo and his brother Vasylko received them with great rejoicing, and kept them for several days asking questions and enjoying their company.

Now it is time to introduce the two brothers.

Princes Danylo and Vasylko

The two princes, - Vasylko and Danylo, - were the princes of the original Kiev Rus principalities.

Vasylko was the Prince of Volhyn and Danylo – the Prince of Galich. These two figures are crucial in Ukrainian history and expose many of Muscovy's fakes.

Danylo of Galich fought in the very first battle against Mongols already in 1223, some 17 years prior to the major invasion. The battle took place at the Kalka river in the present-day Donetsk region. Mstislav of Novgorod (the one from the Lipitsa battle), princes from Kiev, Galich, Volhyn, Chernihiv and Smolensk took part in that battle. There were neither princes, no troops from the Meryan/Rostov-Suzdal land, which is also an illustration in itself of who was the part of the Rus realm and its defenders, and who was not.

The battle ended badly for Rusian troops because their allies, the Cumans, fled the battlefield, but wounded 18-year old Danylo and Vasylko managed to get back to Kiev.

During the Mongol invasion, the two already knew what to expect of the Mongols and managed to defend their princedoms by force and diplomacy quite efficiently. The stories of their bravery spread all over Europe and already in 1249, the Pope offered Danylo the title of the King.

In late 1253 the Pope crowned Danylo of Galich as "Rex Rusiae" or **the King of all Rus**. Thus, the direct legacy to Kiev Rus was confirmed in the eyes of the whole Europe.

The royal crown even established King Danylo's superiority over the princes of the neighboring Catholic countries.

But for Danylo, the title was just the means – in the first place he sought the aid of the Church of Rome to organize a march against the Mongols under the Papal flag. King Danylo specifically informed the Pope that he wanted troops, not a title. There was a rift between King Danylo and the Pope when the latter did not keep his word of providing the troops.

Under Danylo's reign, Galich–Volhyn became one of the most powerful states in east-central Europe. Literature flourished. Demographic growth was enhanced by immigration from the west and the south.

The Kingdom was booming and King Danylo founded new cities. The new cities were built in the western part of the Kingdom to safeguard them from the Mongols raids. One of them was the city of Lviv, officially founded in 1256 and named in honor of Danylo's son, Lev.

King Danylo also founded the city of Kholm even a little more to the West from Lviv and moved the capital of his Kingdom there. The fortress and defenses King Danylo built in that city withstood two fierce sieges by the Mongols. In that city, he died and is buried. It so happened that nowadays Kholm is in present-day Poland, across the border from Lviv.

"The thirteen-century West with its painters and poets and cathedral-builders might have been wiped out by the armed hordes of Jenghis Khan had not Ukraine met and absorbed the shock of onset" - Watson Kirkconnell.

After Danylo's death in 1264, his son Lev succeeded him and moved the capital to Lviv in 1272.

Lithuania ascending

Decades of fighting the Mongols had had its toll, and In 1320, Galich-Volhyn Kingdom became part of the Lithuanian Kingdom. Under the circumstances, it was more like alliance than a conquest.

When one looks at present-day Lithuania on the map, one can hardly believe that for a couple of hundred years it was one of the largest Duchess of Medieval Europe. But it was.

During the 10–11th centuries, Lithuanian territories were among the lands paying tribute to Kiev Rus, and Yaroslav the Wise was the one who invaded Lithuania circa 1040.

In 1219, twenty-one Lithuanian chiefs signed a peace treaty with the Galich and Volhyn principalities. This event is widely accepted as the first proof that the Baltic tribes were uniting and consolidating and those two Rusian principalities – Galich and Volhyn - were the ones who helped Lithuanian tribes to unite.

From the military point of view, Lithuanian tribes learned a lot from two German crusading military orders - the Livonian Brothers of the Sword and the Teutonic Knights who were present on the territory of present-day Latvia. As a matter of fact, the war between the Teutonic Order and Lithuania was one of the longest wars in the history of Europe

For a very short period, Lithuania was a Kingdom too – the same year - 1253, when Danylo of Galich was named the King of Rus, the very same year Lithuanian chief Mindaugas was crowned and the Kingdom of Lithuania was established for the first and only time in Lithuanian history. The day of the Mindaugas coronation is now an official national holiday in Lithuania,- the Statehood Day. With Mindaugas' death, there were no more kings in Lithuanian history.

Although Mindaugas received Christianity, his country remained pagan. Nevertheless, Mindaugas negotiated peace with Galich–Volhyn and married his daughter to Svarn, another son of Danylo of Galich. Svarn will later become Grand Duke of Lithuania.

All this was important to show that there was no enmity between the two states and some Lithuanian Grand Princes were even of the Galich-Volhyn origin.

Lithuania was spared the Mongol invasion because the Mongols were stopped by the dense forests at the eastern borders of present-day Belarus. It means that while Kiev Rus fought the Mongols continuously starting in 1240, Lithuania was gaining power and strength.

In 1242, Minsk became a part of the expanding Grand Duchy of Lithuania. It joined peacefully and local Belarusian elites kept their high rank in the society of the Grand Duchy.

In a very similar manner, the Lithuanian army added Galicia - Volhyn in 1320.

It may appear strange at first, but the motto of the Lithuanian policy was - "We don't destroy the old and don't introduce the new". And following it, the new Lithuanian chief Gediminas pledged not to take away the possessions of the Volhyn nobility and to keep only locals to offices. The Lithuanians also pledged to respect local religious and political practices.

After incorporating Galich-Volhyn, Gediminas moved towards Kiev, where a very important battle took place at the Irpin river, some 15 kilometers to the west of Kiev.

The description of the battle was discovered in the works of Archbishop Georgy Konissky of Belarus, which were published in Moscow in 1846, but written around 1775. Georgy Konissky was also a professor and taught at a Kiev University. Here is his account:

"In 1320 Prince Gediminas came to the land of Rus with his troops and having united forces with Ruthenians who were under command of their leaders Prentseslav, Svitold and Blud together with Gromval, Turnil, Perunad, Ladym and others, drove off the Tatars from Rus, having overcome them in three battles and in the last, the major one, over the Irpin river, where were killed Tymur and Divlat, the Tatar Princes. After these victories, Gedimin renewed the rule of Rus by the people's elected officials, over whom he appointed his representative Prince Olshansky from Ruthenians."

It is important to note that Gediminas joined forces with Ruthenians to free Kiev from the Mongols. (Wikipedia: "Ruthenians and Ruthenes are Latin exonyms formerly used in Western Europe for the ancestors of modern East Slavic peoples, especially the Rus' people with an Eastern Orthodox or Ruthenian Greek Catholic religious background.")

In other words, Ukrainians helped Lithuanians to free Kiev from the Mongols. Ukrainians were elected and were left to rule over Kiev.

Gediminas returned to Lithuania where he founded the city of Vilnius.

The new state's official name was **the Grand Duchy of Lithuania, Ruthenia and Samogitia** (a region in northwestern Lithuania). Gediminas who was a pagan himself, had three or four of his seven sons be baptized as Christian Orthodox, and his daughters married Christians.

But it is only in 1387 Lithuania itself and its princes were finally baptized.

Here is what Timothy Snyder writes in his book *The Reconstruction of Nations: Poland, Ukraine, Lithuania, Belarus, 1569-1999:* "As Lithuanian military power flowed south, to Kyiv, so the civilization of Rus'—Orthodox religion, Church Slavonic language, and mature legal tradition flowed north to Vilnius. Ukraine had provided medieval Lithuania with Christianity and writing."

Believe it or not, but until that time there had been no written Lithuanian language! The Ruthenian/Old Ukrainian language became the most widely spoken language by almost 80% of the population of Lithuania and was used in the official documents of the Grand Duchy until 1697.

Old Ukrainian language also dominated at the Lithuanian court, and it is from Kiev that Lithuania adopted "mature legal tradition" i.e. provisions of administrative, civil, family and criminal laws. These provisions eventually evolved into the Statutes of Lithuania, making the country one of Europe's first rule-of-law states.

S.C. Rowell in his book *Lithuania Ascending* makes the following insightful comment: "Lithuania was a pagan state which carved out a Christian empire but not as the Mongols did. The Tatars ruled over Rus but pressurized its princes from the outside; Lithuanians insinuated themselves into the system of eastern Christendom."

Judging from the last sentence of the quote, it was more like Lithuania became part of Kiev Rus and not vice versa.

Heirs of Rus

Given the facts mentioned above, did Lithuania have the right to call itself the heir of Kiev Rus? Why should there be any heirs of Rus in the first place, if Rus itself stayed alive and continued spreading Christianity and knowledge?

Timothy Snyder views and describes the process this way: "Since Lithuania for a very long time included a majority of Orthodox subjects and most of the Kyivan patrimony, it was called a "Rusian" realm. In unifying his domains with Poland in 1385, (king) Jogaila acted as "Grand Duke of Lithuania and Lord and Heir of Rus'…

In a **1449 treaty** between Poland-Lithuania and Muscovy, the former was called "**Rusian**," the latter "**Muscovite.**"

As can be seen, by the middle of the 15th century two distinctly different realms had been formed. One was officially called Rusian (with a single "s"), another – Muscovite, with Muscovy being the name used in the official documents, such as the treaty.

There was no "Russia".

There were the "heirs of Rus" which were Lithuania (including Belarus and major part of Ukraine) and Poland.

Muscovy was not among them.

Russian Orthodoxy – Third Rome or New Sarai?

Kiev Rus realm was baptized into Christianity by Vladimir the Great in 988 (Kiev) and 989 (Novgorod).

How and when did the future Muscovy receive Christianity?

Christianity in Moxel

As quoted in the chapter about Moxel, William Rubruck defined the people of that land as pagans even in 1254. There were bishops in that land starting 1073, but their fates were mostly tragic. Like the destiny of bishop Leontiy who was killed that very year, he came to that area. Bishop Nestor was expelled by Andrey Bogolyubsky in 1156. Bishop Leon was expelled in 1158. Bishop Feodor Kaluger in 1172 for his cruelty had his right hand chopped off, had his tongue cut out, was blinded and drowned in a swamp.

Everything changed with the Mongol invasion.

Golden Horde's yarlyks, Sarai eparchy

The Mongols found Orthodox religion potentially useful in keeping their subjects in control.

William Rubruck on his way back from Mongolia in 1255 writes the following: "He (Nestorian priest) was making, by order of Sartak, a big church and a new village on the west bank of the (Volga) river, and wanted, he said, to make books for Sartak's use. I know, however, that Sartak cares not for such things. Sarai and the palace of Batu are on the eastern shore."

Five years later, in 1260, Orthodox eparchy was established at Sarai.

Donald Ostrowski in his book *Muscovy and the Mongols: Cross-Cultural Influences on the Steppe Frontier* provides the logic behind this move: "The bishop of that (Sarai) eparchy, while in residence in Sarai, had three main functions: (1) to deal diplomatically with the government of the Qipchaq Khanate; (2) to act as a liaison between Sarai and Constantinople; (3) to attend to the religious needs of Christian merchants, as well as those of the grand prince, and his entourage, when the grand prince attended his sovereign, the Qipchaq khan, in Sarai.".

It may be a shocking revelation for many readers, but Muscovy bishops were receiving the permission at Sarai too to take their position. The permissions were called *yarlyks*.

Yarlyks were also issued to Muscovite tsars and demonstrated the vassal state of modern Russia to the Golden Horde for a much longer period than the Russians want modern people to know.

The facts and documents about the yarlyks were so many, that even Catherine II had to admit their existence.

The very first yarlyk found by historians was issued by Mengu-Timur to Metropolitan Kirill for the bishopric in Tver in 1267.

There are six yarlyks stored in the Moscow metropolitan museum, although there were seven yarlyks in all.

Rift with Constantinople, loss of canonicity

Until 1439, Moscow bishops were required to receive yarlyks first at Sarai and only after that they had the right to go to Constantinople for approval. Starting in 1441, Constantinople refused to continue this practice. Seven years later, in 1448, Moscow decided not to bother with further approvals and on December 15, 1448, a council of bishops chose Iona as metropolitan without the official approval of the Patriarch of Constantinople.

That is when the canonicity of the future Russian Orthodox Church ended.

Donald Ostrowski writes of an interesting episode: "Muscovite chronicles of the end of the fifteenth century and sixteenth century contain the statement that Iona had gone to Constantinople, where the patriarch had given Iona his blessing to become metropolitan after Isidor, But, as Lur'e pointed out, this entry must be considered a later interpolation entered into the Muscovite chronicles to provide legitimacy for Iona's usurpation of the metropolitanate. Iona's testament, for example, does not mention any such trip to Constantinople, although we can expect that it would if such a trip had occurred."

"A later interpolation entered into the Muscovite chronicles to provide legitimacy" is something one should be aware of constantly when reading the "Russian" narrative of its history. Even chronicles were altered and forged!

We will explore another case of such "interpolation" in the following chapter.

Third Rome ambition

1448 is the year of the Treaty mentioned in the previous chapter when Muscovy was still named Muscovy, remember? What changed and how and why did Muscovy decide to become "Russia"?

We will continue to quote Timothy Snyder: "After the fall of Constantinople to the Turks in 1453, Muscovy espoused spiritual and political claims as the seat of Orthodoxy, the heir of Byzantium, and the successor of Kyivan Rus'."

Here is the answer – Muscovy decided to replace Constantinople! It did not care to call itself Muscovy until it saw the chance to take the seat of Orthodoxy! Is vanity a sin?

The major problem was the question of legacy and succession. And here is the path Muscovy chose:

"These provided the justification for Muscovy's wars with their fellow East Slavs of Lithuania, whose grand dukes had regarded themselves for a century as the successors of Kyivan princes. In practice, Muscovy's claim to be Rus' pushed Lithuania toward Poland. When Ivan IV (the Terrible, reigned 1530-1584, proclaimed tsar 1547) began the Livonian Wars in 1558, he hastened the Polish-Lithuanian Union of 1569. At that time, of course, Poland-Lithuania also claimed to be Rus'."

Muscovy needed Kiev Rus' legacy so bad, it started the wars with Lithuania, Poland, and Sweden for the name "Rus"!

Around 1547 the bishop of the Don and Sarai was recalled officially from Sarai and was set up in Krutitsk, a suburb of Moscow.

Donald Ostrowski again: "Important aspects of this new ideology were the replacement of the Byzantine basileus as the protector of the Church by the Muscovite ruler and the defining of the Muscovite's authority in terms that had been applied to the Byzantine basileus. Another important aspect was the creation of a virtual past that designated Muscovy as the true inheritor of Kievan Rus, as well as of Byzantium. This new virtual past also worked to deny Muscovy's status as the inheritor of the Tatar Khanate of Qipchaq."

Peter I and the Synod

Peter I continued the trend. Here is how the British religious press described what happened with Muscovy Church during Peter's reign:

"From the days of Peter the Great, the established Church had been not only in fact but openly and formally controlled by the Autocracy. Peter suppressed the last vestiges of its freedom by abolishing the Patriarchate and substituting a Procuratorship of the Holy Synod. The ecclesiastical members of the Synod were royal nominees destitute of power: the Procurator --a lawyer appointed by and directly responsible to the Czar— possessed and exercised the entire executive -authority… the Orthodox Church and this control were so constant and effective that the Church could be regarded as little more than a branch of the Civil Service. As an institution, it was characterized by an unintelligent anti-democratic outlook and a slavish subservience to the Romanoff dynasty."

Partitions of Poland by Catherine II

Here is what a former Putin's advisor, but currently his ardent critic Andrei Illarionov wrote in 2018 during the times of the Ukrainian church gaining back its independent status:

"Three partitions of Rzeczpospolita (Polish state) Catherine II justified by her claims on "grandfathers' legacy" flowing allegedly from the Orthodox believers' subjection of former Kiev metropolis to Moscow."

Stalin's order for the Russian Church

After the Bolshevik Revolution of 1917 when the church was forbidden and many cathedrals were ruined, the Russian Orthodox Church was revived by the order of Stalin on September 4, 1943, when he needed to mobilize his people for the war. Basically, that purpose stayed with that organization since its very inception in the early thirteenth century.

Ukrainian Church Independence & Putin's Security Council

Official Constantinople's statement before granting Autocephaly in 2018:

"Already from the early 14thcentury, when the see of the Kyivan Metropolis was moved without the canonical permission of the Mother Church to Moscow, there have been tireless efforts on the part of our Kyivan brothers for independence from ecclesiastical control by the Moscow center."

The day Ukrainian Church received Autocephaly in 2018, the very same day Putin gathered his Security Council. What could be so important for one country's security in another country's Church receiving a different status?

Can anyone imagine, for example, President of the United States gathering his or her Security Council if, for example, Britain decided to become Catholic again? Very hard to imagine, is it not?

So, what is the true reason behind Moscow's fear for its security in this case? There was no immediate threat to "Russian Orthodox believers" in Ukraine to start planning their defenses especially after the four previous years on defending "the Russian speakers" in Donbas. Besides, the Church in Russia, at least nominally, is considered separate from the State.

So, what was it after all? What could be the reason?

The reason has been the same since the middle of the fifteenth century and for almost six hundred years already – to uphold "a virtual past" that "designated Muscovy as the true inheritor of Kievan Rus."

Moscow rulers understand quite well, that if this virtual reality crumbles, all the forgeries and fakes will be exposed.

All the claims on the glorious past of Rus-Ukraine will be debunked including the claims on Crimea as "the cradle of Russian faith."

There will be no more cover-ups for the wars of expansion under the pretense of some "defenses" past and present.

The system will return to its "default" status, and the whole world will see Muscovy' as the direct inheritor of the Tatar Khanate of Qipchaq of the Golden Horde.

The Song of Igor's Campaign, Vladimir Nabokov

"The *Song* alone of all Old Russian literature has become a national classic, one that is familiar to every educated Russian. An English translation of it by Vladimir Nabokov was published in 1960," says Wikipedia. But does Russia have anything to do with the literary masterpiece?

Vladimir Nabokov graduated with honors in Slavic and French from Cambridge University, England. He came to the United States in 1940 and became an American citizen. Some of his best-known novels in English are Lolita, Bend Sinister, and a critical biography Nikolai Gogol. In a rather extensive foreword he says the following:

"According to the annals of Kiev Rus, a territorial prince Igor with throne town in Novgorod-Siversk near Chernihiv in present-day Ukraine, moved by a vision, set out on Tuesday, April 23, 1185, for the steppes beyond the river Donets to fight the Cumans."

It is the same Cumans, who will be allies to Rus in less 38 years and who will cause the defeat in the battle at the Kalka river in 1223. Even the places of the two battles will be very close to each other and in the same region of the present-day Donetsk oblast.

The Song manuscript was bought accidentally around 1790 by a high-ranking member of the Synod Count Aleksey Musin-Pushkin.

Vladimir Nabokov, being a distinguished writer himself, writes the following: "Magnificent literary masterpiece, half-poem, half oration, henceforth to be known as *The Slovo o Polku Igoreve*, The *Tale of Igor's Campaign*.

But it is only in 1864, "the lovers of Russian letters... learned that not only had a great bard flourished in Russia at the end of the twelfth century but that he had had a predecessor named Boyan in the eleventh."

"The Song... is a harmonious, many-leveled, many-hued, uniquely poetical structure created in a sustained and controlled surge of inspiration by an artist with a fondness for pagan gods and percipience of sensuous things.

It is the lucid work of one man, not the random thrum of a people. From the extraordinary prelude... to the conclusion of the work,... there is a constant interplay of themes and mutual echoes."

And continues: "Especially satisfying to one's sense of inner concord and unity is the ample treatment of the theme of the Rivers, among which the Great Don plays a leading role... Igor does not attain the blue mirage of the Don,... but in a perfect structural move the artist substitutes for the Great Don, the "little" Donets, with which, or rather with whom, the prince in the Liberation part of The Song indulges in a charming colloquy... Igor's speech of thanks to the Lesser Don (Donets) is beautifully duplicated by his wife's prayer to the Dnepr: the great Kievan river transmits as it were the power of intercession and assistance to the prairie stream."

"...through the mist of Scandinavian sagas certain bridges or ruins of bridges may be distinguished linking Scottish-Gaelic romances with Kievan ones."

The Song demonstrates the coexistence between Christianity and the ancient Slavic religion. For example, Igor's wife Yaroslavna invokes natural forces from the walls of the city of Putyvl. Christian motifs are presented along with pagan gods and vivid artistic images.

The Song is often compared to other national epics, such as The Song of Roland and The Song of the Nibelungs, but it differs from them by its numerous descriptions of nature and the mysterious role it plays in human lives.

"As things stand, one masterpiece not only lords it over Kievan letters but rivals the greatest European poems of its day," – sums up Vladimir Nabokov.

How The Song was discovered

"The actual text discovered by Musin-Pushkin was a much later transcript made, it is conjectured, in the sixteenth century.., by a monastic scribe. "

"The precious manuscript of The Slovo perished during the Moscow conflagration of 1812 when Musin's house was burned to the ground. All we possess in the way of basic material is the edition of 1800 and an apograph that in 1795 or 1796 Count Musin-Pushkin had a scribe make from the Manuscript for Empress Catherine II. This Apograph (known as the Archivniy, or Ekaterininskiy Spisok), which differs only in a few insignificant details from the editio princeps, was discovered among Catherine's papers more than six decades later by the historian Pekarski, who published it in 1964 in an Appendix 2 to volume V, 1862, of Zapiski Imperatorsoy Academy of Sciences).

It was during the preparation of the Apograph and of three or four additional copies (now lost) that the news of Musin's remarkable acquisition spread among the lovers of Russian letters. They learned that not only had a great bard flourished in Russia at the end of the twelfth century but that he had had a predecessor named Boyan in the eleventh. Of the author of The Song, we do not know the name but we know the work."

The date of the actual composition of The Song can be established more precisely than that of most European epics of the twelfth century (and Nabokov names the end of 1187). As for the "human form of a poet", Nabokov thinks it is reasonable to suppose that the bard was a Kievan knight, or a learned monk "taking a pagan vacation", but that he was evidently "a keen sportsman" with a fine knowledge of steppe fauna and flora who may have taken part in Igor's campaign personally.

Language

Nabokov thinks that the author of The Song was either Kievan knight or a learned monk living in that area of present-day Ukraine, but insists that the text was written in some "Old Russian" language. Is it so?

Using the term "Old-Russian" means that there was "Old Russia" which is very misleading. There was Rus with the capital in Kiev and according to simple logic, the language of that country should be "Old Rusian" with the single "s" at least. Sometimes this language is called Ruthenian. The Song was written in the language Kiev and its realm were speaking. Was it the same language Suzdal land was speaking? (There was not Moscow on the map in those days yet.)

During that time – the end of the twelfth century – the core area of the future Russia corresponding to the present-day Golden Ring area around Moscow was populated by the Meryan tribe as proven by archeological research by Count Alexey Uvarov. The spoken language of the Volga Finns populating that area could only be "Old Finnish." Russian historian Dmitry Korsakov in his book *Merya and Rostov Princedom* published in 1872 in Kazan, states that it is Rostov-Suzdal land populated by the Finnish tribes was the land where "the Greater Russian" tribe was formed.

A Kiev prince Yury Dolgorukiy who had come to that land some fifty years before The Song was written, definitely spoke the same language as the literary masterpiece, but Dolgorukiy was a stranger in that land and was later expelled by his own son born in that land to a local mother. You will have the opportunity to see the looks of this son below. But back to the language issue.

The previous chapter showed the way the Grand Duchy of Lithuania received the spoken and written language from Kiev in 1320 and what language it was. It can be called Old Ukrainian, although historians call it Chancery Slavonic. Here is how that language was perceived in Muscovy:

Timothy Snyder in his book *The Reconstruction of Nations*: "In Muscovy, the state language of the Grand Duchy of Lithuania, which we are calling "Chancery Slavonic," was called "Lithuanian" or Belorussian." Although modern Russian historians sometimes call this language "Russian," at the time Muscovite scribes had to translate the Lithuanian statutes into Moscow dialect for them to be of use to their court".

There are so many facts in this single quote. While Kiev educated Lithuania, Lithuania educated Muscovy. And even in the fifteenth century Muscovites had to translate the language which some of the "modern historians call "Russian"!

Musin-Pushkin and A. Malinovsky could not understand even the copy of the manuscript of The Song which was written by the Kievan cursive of the seventeenth century. For example, at first, they decided that the poem deals with the victorious campaign of Rus princes against Cumans in 1103. "There are so many Little Russian (Ukrainian) words in it, that for anyone who does not know the language it is impossible to understand it" – complained Musin-Pushkin in his correspondence.

The manuscript was read and transliterated in 1794-1795 by Mykola Bantysh-Kamensky, a Ukrainian scientist, and a graduate of Kiev-Mohyla Academy in Kiev. At the time of translation, he was a director of the Moscow Archives.

Ukrainian nuances. Buy Tur

Vladimir Nabokov mentions one example when understanding The Song without knowing Ukrainian language and nature is hard:

"The names Buy Tur, Wild Bull or Turbulent Aurochs, and Yar Tur, Fierce Bull or Ardent Aurochs, as applied to Vsevolod (of Chernihiv) have struck nonbelievers in the authenticity of the Song as Americanisms of the late eighteenth century imported into Russia via France. Tur may mean either of the two species of Bos, the real tur, urus, Bos primigenus (from which the domestic ox has been evolved) and the zubr, aurochs, Bison bonasus. By the twelfth century, the primigenial bull was extinct but aurochs occurred in southern Russia up to the eighteenth century and symbolized courage and strength. On the other hand, the word tur has consistently been applied in the Ukraine to a large gray form of a domestic bull."

It is about Igor's brother Vsevolod Svyatoslavovich, not Vsevolod of Suzdal. He died in 1196 and was buried in Chernihiv. After World War Two, the scientists discovered his grave and Moscow Academician Mikhail Gerasimov using the forensic sculpture technique based on the skull reconstructed the face of Vsevolod the Buy Tur. The skeleton was of a person of immense power. You can see the result of the reconstruction above.

The Hins or Khynova

There was one nationality mentioned in The Song, which caused many troubles to Kiev Rus land, Nabokov translates their name as the "Hins". In other translations, their name is the "Khynova."

"On the river Kayla

Darkness has covered the light.

Over the Russian land

The Kumans have spread,

Like a brood of pards,

And great turbulence

Imparted to the Hin"

For you have iron breastplates

Under Latin helmets;

And many nations – Hins, Lithuanians, Yatvangians,

Dermners, and Kumans –

Have dropped their spears

And bowed their heads

Beneath those steel swords

They were quite a treacherous group of people providing weapons to the dark forces attacking Igor's regiment. Here is part of Igor's wife's prayer in Chernihiv:

"Wind, Great Wind!

Why, lord, blow perversely?

Why carry those Hinish dartlets

On your light winglets

Against my husband's warriors"

Nabokov guesses that the Hin stood for "the name, a nonce word, probably applies to the entire group of Asiatic tribes known to the Russians." It is quite strange that making such a supposition in 1960, Nabokov fails to mention that already in 1914, Russian linguist Vsevolod Miller in his work *"Khynova" of The Slovo o Polku Igoreve* had proven that under the "Hins" the author of the Song meant the Fins, the people of the Meryan land under the rule of Vsevolod the Big Nest of Suzdal.

There is this passage in the Song which appears in the opposition to that conclusion:

"Now in Rim [people] scream

Under Kuman sabers,

And Volodymir [screams]

Under wounding blows.

Woe and anguish to you, [Volodymyr]

Great prince Vsevolod!

Do you not think of flying from afar

To safeguard the paternal throne?

Nabokov comments that it is Vsevolod of Vladimir, a town in the Suzdal region, surnamed The Big Nest. He also thinks that this prince was perhaps the most powerful one among the descendants of Vladimir Monomachus of Kiev, his grandfather.

But on careful examination, some questions arise. How natural is it to call on somebody to safeguard a throne when not a throne is at stake? Even more important question is – which paternal throne it was – in Pereyaslav or Kiev, and what right did Vsevolod have for that throne to safeguard it?

Yury Dolgorukiy's branch of the Rurik's family

Let us look closer at the whole Suzdal branch of the Rurik line who, according to the Russian historians, are the "true heirs of Kiev Rus."

This Vsevolod was the tenth or even eleventh son of Yuri Dolgorukiy and was named The Big Nest because he had many children himself. Two of his sons will be Yuri and Yaroslav, who in 30 years will lead the troops into the slaughter of the Lipitsa battle.

208

Later on Yuri (Vsevolod's son and Dolgorukiy's grandson) will fight on the side of the Mongols and die in one of the battles in Germany.

Yaroslav will become the one who will fail to show for the Battle at the Kalka river in 1223. This Yaroslav will become the father of Alexander "Nevsky." He will serve the Mongols well until the time he gets poisoned in Karakorum in Mongolia of which event William Rubruck reported in his work.

In 1177, only 8 years before Igor's campaign, Vsevolod the Big Nest ruined Ryazan with the help of the Cuman allies. The same Cumans Igor was fighting in the Song.

But all of this started with Vsevolod's father, Yuri Dolgorukiy who was born into the second marriage of Kiev Great Prince Vladimir Monomachus who already had five sons from his first marriage with Gytha, the daughter of the English king Harold II. It means that from his earliest years, Yuri Dolgorukiy had little hope for a good inheritance, not to mention hope for the throne.

Vladimir Nabokov may not have known, but together with the copy of "The Song" among the papers of Catherine II, her "Reflections on the Project of History of Russia" written in French was discovered. A.F. Bychkov printed it in 1873 in St. Petersburg. In it, among other things, Catherine II wrote down her thoughts on Yuri Dolgorukiy:

"Of all the princes, the most prone to mistakes before the Tatar coming was, in my opinion, surely Yury Dolgorukiy, son of Vladimir II: not receiving Volhyn and Galich in inheritance, he haunted other princes incessantly, turning them one against another... He was expelled to the Kliazma river..: he built several cities there and named them by the names of the cities he was denied on Volhyn, and, among others, he named the place in which he settled Vladimir because Vladimir (original) was the capital of Volhyn..."

Correction – the city's original name was Volodymyr because that is how in reality the name of the Kiev ruler was – Volodymyr the

Great. That is how they are still spelled in Ukrainian transcription. Yury Dolgorukiy did not found Moscow – that little wooden village will first be mentioned around 1272.

Yury Dolgorukiy did not have much time for creative work – almost all the time he devoted himself to plotting and trying to get what he thought belonged to him. Historians counted that he alone made 12 assaults on Rus, some of them in alliance with the Cumans. No wonder that when in 1157 Yury Dolgorukiy returned to Kiev, he was poisoned – the Kievans could not forgive him his raids.

Yuri's first son from a Cuman woman Andrey Bogolyubsky continued his father's efforts and tried to make raids into Rus land. (Andrey's face reconstructed by the same M. Gerasimov mentioned above, is a good illustration that Bogolyubsky's mother's Asian genes must have prevailed by the way).

The Song exposes myths

Here is what Wikipedia says about Bogolyubsky: "His reign saw a complete decline of Kiev's rule over northeastern Rus and the rise of Vladimir as the new capital city. Andrei was known in the West as *Scythian Caesar*, and is beatified as a saint in the Russian Orthodox Church... In 1169 his troops sacked Kiev, devastating it as never before...plundering the city, stealing much religious artwork, which included the Byzantine "*Mother of God*" icon."

Wow! How is that? If Kiev had seen "a complete decline" and had been "sacked" and devastated as "never before", how is it so beautiful and powerful in the historically correct The Song of Igor's Campaign sixteen years later? Why does the author of The Song fail to mention such a tragedy?

210

The answer is simple – it never happened. How do we know it for sure? We know it because at the beginning of that year (February 25, 1169) Andrey Bogolyubsky tried to attack the Great Novgorod, but lost 12,000 of his troops. To endeavor on another military campaign the same year on a much stronger Kiev would have been impossible and suicidal for sure for the rest of the troops.

Bogolyubsky did try approaching Kiev in 1174, but his troops were dispersed already on the march to Vyshgorod, Kiev's satellite city to the north.

The question arises of who would want to create such fake and why?

Someone who needed Kiev to cease being the capital. Someone who would be interested to see the center of power shifted to the future Muscovy. And not just civilian power, but the religious too signified by the Byzantine's icon, the symbol of metropolis and legacy to be a center of Orthodox religion? But here we read in the last verse of The Song:

"Igor rides up the Borichev [slope in Kiev]

To the Blessed Virgin of the Tower,

Countries rejoice,

Cities are merry"

"Blessed Virgin of the Tower" is that icon and, as can be seen, it is in Kiev in 1185.

In symbolic, even Christian sense, it means that Igor, after the trial, ascends (rides up) to receive a blessing to become a new ruler of Kiev Rus.

The author of The Song is very clear that it is Igor of Chernihiv is the successor of Kiev throne and not Vsevolod of Suzdal: "Hard as it is for the head to be without shoulders; bad it is for the body to be without head; for the Rusian land to be without Igor."

(Igor was not destined to succeed the Kiev throne though – he will succeed the Chernihiv one. The next ruler of Kiev Rus became Rurik Rostislavovich who, being an inveterate hunter, in 1193 established a hunting lodge some 100 kilometers to the north of Kiev and named it Chernobyl.)

Historians report that there was a big stir in Russia after The Song was published, because of such an ending and because of how powerful and in full glory Kiev is portrayed in the times when it was supposed to be "in shambles." The stir was so big that even Karmazin had to invent a theory of two different icons.

Anyway, who could be behind all those falsifications about Yury Dolgorukiy and his fake founding of Moscow in 1147? About Andrey Bogolyubsky and his ruining Kiev and stealing the important icon? About "the paternal throne" for Vsevolod the Big Nest? It could have been only someone with state vision and enough state power to implement that vision of the forged history.

Catherine's copy of The Song

It is now known that Catherine II had a special committee working under her command on that "project of the history of Russia," and Musin-Pushkin who purchased The Song was part of that commission and acted on Catherine's order to look for all valuable documents and papers everywhere starting with the monasteries.

The copy of the Song found among Catherine's papers after her death Vladimir Nabokov mentions, was not a copy, but more like a working paper with notes and references. It was more like the work of continuous translation and composition in progress. Judging by the type of paper – and it was the Dutch paper "Pro Patria" produced in 1792 - Catherine II may have worked and made alterations to the text for four years until her death in 1796. The passage about Vsevolod and his "safeguarding of the paternal throne" was very likely added by Catherine II or her commission.

Catherine II died in 1796, but Musin-Pushkin decided to have The Song published only in 1800. We could check and see if there were any corrections or insertions made, but Moscow authorities say that both the original and the first copy burnt in the Moscow fire of 1812. This also raises some questions since the preparations to burn Moscow lasted several days and they had time to evacuate the most valuable archives and libraries.

Conspiracy theory

At approximately the same time The Song was published, there appeared Zadonshchina poem very resembling The Song in narrative and style, but already about Dmitry Donskoi and his fighting the Mongols.

Here is how Vladimir Nabokov characterized it: "Zadonshchina (is) a vulgar imitation of the Song... and belongs to the coarse and ponderously didactic Moscow era which succeeded the marvelously artistic Kievan one. The Zadonshchina differs from the Song of Igor as sackcloth from samite."

Is it possible it was planned by Catherine II to substitute The Song? With all the crimes Catherine II committed against Ukraine, (and we recall her ruining the Zaporozh Sich and deporting the Cossacks to the Kuban), it cannot be excluded. Her death surely brought relief for some time to Ukraine and may have saved the precious literary masterpiece.

The Song and nowadays

Answering the question at the beginning of this chapter of whether The Song is about Russia, the answer will be – yes, but not in the way Russia would like it to be. It is on the side of the ominous force threatening to occupy Rus-Ukraine. And what is even worse, it does so not openly, but in a mean way instigating others (Cumans in this case), and secretly supplying them with the weaponry.

It is so symbolic that as these lines are being written, in the same very place where Igor fought his battle some 834 years before, a similar battle is taking place. And although it is bullets and shells now instead of dartlets and arrows, the supplier is the same. It is surely a battle not for territory, or anything else – it is the battle for the legacy of Kiev Rus and self-defense of an ancient Rus nation.

If one listens to the current claims Russia makes, one can easily distinguish the same claims Yuri Dolgorukiy was making centuries ago.

Nabokov, Karamzin, Uvarov

"Nabokov was born on 22 April 1899 (10 April 1899 Old Style), in Saint Petersburg, to a wealthy and prominent family of the Russian nobility that traced its roots to the 14th-century Tatar prince Nabok Murza" – Wikipedia.

Historian Nickolai Karmazin was a descendant of a Tatarian prince Kara-Murza ("black prince").

"Uvarovs, Russian nobility, descend from Minchak Kasayev who arrived from the Golden Horde… was Christened as Simeon; he had children: David, Zloba, Orchan who were later renamed into Orynka and Uvar. From them descended: the Davydovs, the Minchakovs, the Zlobins, the Oreshkins, and from Uvar – the Uvarovs. (Referential Encyclopedic Dictionary by K. Krai, St. Petersburg 1848, p. 589)

The Three Bogatyrs Painting by Vasnetsov

If this famous painting by Viktor Vasnetsov was a photographic picture, it would be taken somewhere in the proximity of Kiev. And the dates would be somewhere around the tenth - eleventh century.

The characters portrayed are called bogatyrs or knight-errants who appear in Kiev Rus' epic poems as warriors of immense strength and courage defending Rus from the enemies.

The painting portrays the most notable bogatyrs: Alyosha Popovich, Dobrynya Nikitich and Ilya Muromets. Although some of their adventures are fictional, and even exceed in imagination modern "Game of Thrones" (the dragons in the epic poems have mostly three heads which could even grow back immediately, imagine that!), the characters of the bogatyrs themselves were based on real people.

According to the Kievan chronicles, **Dobrynya Nikitich** was from the Volyhn region, the land to the West from Kiev where Friar de Carpini will meet Vassylko and Danylo of Galich. Danylo's sister Malysha was a housekeeper at the court of the famous Queen Olga of Kiev. It is Malysha who became the mother of Volodymir the Great (the Baptizer).

Alyosha Popovich was born in Pyriatyn city in Poltava region, not far from the place where several hundred years later the world-famous wrestler Ivan Poddubny will be born too. The great Ukrainian poet Taras Shevchenko, while in that area wrote a poem "A thought about Oleksiy Popovich from Pyriatyn'.

Ilya Muromets' last name sounds like Murom, a place in present-day Russia. But that city is highly unlikely to be his home town for several reasons. First, Murom was in the Meryan land and we now know that there was almost no interaction between Kiev and people in that area. Second, what kind of warriors were the people of that land was demonstrated during the Lipitza Battle mentioned in one of the previous chapters. And third, in one of the chronicles, it is mentioned that Ilya's home was one day's distance from Kiev, and Murom is 1,200 kilometers away. There is a village Morivsk in Chernihiv region north of Kiev which fits the description perfectly, and the historians think that Ilya's last name was Morivets. Chernihiv is the city where Igor and Vsevolod Buy Tur from *The Tale of Igor's Campaign* were from and it is well possible that the three may have been even distantly related. Who and why wanted to change his last name into Muromets can be guessed easily.

The chronicles suggest that the Ilya spent 33 years home with his lower part of the body being paralyzed. After he got mysteriously cured, Ilya went to defend Kiev. After many years of military service, he decided to become a monk at the Kiev-Pechersk monastery. He died and was buried there.

Austrian diplomat in his *Diary of Erich Lassota: Habsburg and Zaporozhian Cossacks*, mentions Ilya's grave while traveling through Kiev in 1594. (Erich was on a diplomatic mission sent by the Habsburg dynasty in an attempt to enlist the Zaporozhian Cossacks into the imperial service). Only Lassota reports that Ilya's grave was at St. Sophia Cathedral at the time and not in Kiev-Pechersk Monastery.

In 1988, Ilya's remains were analyzed by scientists. The analysis showed that the remains belonged to a man of 177 cm height which was above average at that time. It showed an inborn spine defect and traces of battle wounds suggesting that Ilya was probably killed during one of the many sieges of Kiev.

To summarize, all the three "Russian" heroes were in reality Ukrainians (Ruthenians) defending their homeland – Rus and its capital – Kiev.

Made in the USA
Middletown, DE
14 December 2019